MW01089328

Choosing A Godly Mate

ISBN-10: 1975726995
ISBN-13: 978-1975726997

For Worldwide Distribution, Printed in the U.S.A.

Choosing A Godly Mate

How to Find The Real Deal Before Saying 'I Do'

Nelson L. Schuman

Dedication

To all those who desire to marry a mate who will love, treasure, respect and support them for a lifetime, as Christ loved the church

Endorsements

"What I love most about Nelson Schuman is the authenticity, honesty, and transparency he carries not only in the realms of deliverance, but in his personal experiences and what he has had to walk through to get to where he is now in his life and ministry. I have had the opportunity to witness firsthand the hand of God upon his ministry, and when you listen to his heart and testimony of where God has brought him from, one cannot help but realize that what he is teaching and the place he is ministering from, are places Nelson has actually lived through. It is a great honor and privilege for me to write this endorsement knowing that his newest book on finding a godly mate will dismantle the lies of the enemy and expose the demonic realm's attempts to thwart God's person of destiny, for both men and women alike. In his book, Choosing A Godly Mate, Nelson deals with the foundational issues of what to look for in a godly tentative spouse, what to do in the waiting, safeguards that can help along the way, sound biblical teaching on staying in alignment with the Lord and with heaven through that process, all the while exposing some of the most prevalent demonic spirits and entities that are attacking marriages, potential marriages, and relationships overall. I highly recommend this book to all who are hungering and desiring to go past the surface and into the depths of the

realm of the spirit to know what is at the root of so much of what we see in people, in marriages, and in relationships today. This book will not only teach, train, and equip the reader, but will bring about countless blessings to those who put them into use."

Kevin Stevens, Apostolic Leader
Greater Glory Revival Center/Ministries
Destiny Prophets (Inner Healing and Deliverance Coaching)
Brockport, N.Y.

"Choosing a Godly Mate" is a must read book that will benefit not only those who are single, but married couples as well. Author, Nelson Schuman, provides rich insight and a fantastic balance of deep spiritual truths along with solid, practical wisdom."

Robia Scott – author of Counterfeit Comforts: Freedom From the Imposters that Keep you from True Peace, Purpose and Passion.,
Aliso Viejo, CA

"Far too many couples in this world have no idea how their mothers and fathers affected their views, behaviors and future living. The enemy is real and whispers to couples every day causing them to have real conflict. Every person who wants to be married needs to read this book and get set free from tormenting spirits that have had a right to them since childhood."

Tim Brown – Sr. Pastor, New Life Assembly of God, Noblesville, IN

Testimonies

"Choosing A Godly Mate is a book that helps people to look at themselves first to be set free from all past wounds, delivered from any enemy spirits that have controlled them in order to be unencumbered to be married to a healthy mate instead of being drawn into a co-dependent relationship set up for failure at the start."

"If only I had read this book before I got married the first time, I would not have gone through three marriages that have all been horrible. Thank you Nelson for revealing the truth to the world."

"Every church and school in the world needs to have people who want to be married read Choosing A Godly Mate first. It would save a lot of time and money in divorce courts as people would not be visiting the courts and enjoying their spouses the way God intended."

"I am a woman who is 50 years old. I thought I was crazy when my previous husbands treated me so horribly and yet blamed me for the divorces. Now I finally know what I have been dealing with. The enemy is so sneaky and evil but no more will I be deceived."

"So many people in the church have no idea how the enemy has caused so much havoc in their marriages and ministries. When you get set free from demonic spirits you can live in peace and joy and actually love your spouse the way Christ loved the church. Thank you for writing the revelation in this book Nelson!"

"I have been waiting for someone to finally explain what has been going on in my marriages of the past that have failed. Finally I know the truth. I got tired of looking at myself in the mirror while the enemy in me wanted to blame my wives for the strife. It was the Jezebel spirit in me the whole time. I am so sorry Lord, please forgive me as I repent from my past and turn completely to you."

"Every school in the world needs to require this to be read before they graduate. Every church in the world needs to have this book as pre-marriage counseling guidance. It is time to stop the increase in divorce and start to see Christians being real. Thank you Lord!"

"I wish I would have read this book when I was 15 instead of 58. I would have had a much different life that would have seen so much more peace in my marriages. Thank you God for the revelation in Choosing A Godly Mate. I am going to give this book to all of my children."

"If everyone would read this book we would see love and peace returning to the marriages in this world. The voices that people are hearing in their heads are all demonic spirits which control people like puppets. The enemy world is real and active and Choosing A Godly Mate helps expose the tactics of the enemy."

"I now know what the problems have been in our family and why so many of my siblings have gone through divorces. Thank you Lord for revealing the truth."

Acknowledgements

I want to thank all who have supported me in the ministry of getting people set free from the enemy in order to allow them to make wise decisions and live a life full of peace, love and joy. It is truly a privilege to see the lives of thousands around the world changing their lives, saving their marriages and purifying ministries. God wants His people to be in unity in marriage and it is time to go on the offensive and no longer allow the enemy to deceive.

A special thank you to my dear friend, Tina Marie Kirkpatrick, for the amazing dedication of editing my book with such priority while in the midst of Hurricane Harvey. The Holy Spirit's guidance during your review was truly evident. We share a common bond in growing up in Columbia City, IN as you unknowingly drove past the farm where I grew up many times on U.S. Highway 30 to visit your best friend Leah, who lived across the road from me. You are truly an awesome friend, great partner in ministry, amazing editor and your humor is truly epic. God has brought us together for such a time as this to help those hurting in relationships around the world. You rock!

I want to especially thank all of my family and friends who the Lord has brought into my life who truly love me unconditionally and know my heart and compassion to help people with all I am capable of through Christ to live a life aligned with the power and love of the Lord. You are all awesome and I love you for your support and dedication:

(Aggie, April, Ashley, Austin, Becca, Bill, Bob, Brandon, Brian, C, Carrie, Cassia, Cindy, Charles, Chris, Christy, Chuck, Courtney, Crystle, Dan, Daniel, David, Dawn, Dean, Deborah, Dianna, Duane, Elaine, Erin, Garry, George, Gina, Hannah, Karen, Keith, James, Jan, Jana, Jenny, Jess, Jessica, Joe, John, Jordan, Judy, Julie, Larry, Lisa, Luke, Marshall, Marvin, Megan, Michael, Michelle, Misty, Neil, Nick, Nova, Owen, Patti, Patty, Paul, Phil, Priscilla, Randy, Remon, Robia, Ron, Scot, Sharell, Steve, Sue, Taylor, Tina, Todd, Trond, Tyler, and Tim)

Table of Contents

Introduction

So many people in the world simply want to be loved unconditionally by another person in a committed and trusted marriage for a lifetime. Unfortunately, most people have been hurt when growing up in their childhoods by fathers or mothers who were not present, distant, unloving, critical, controlling, or at the worst case of the spectrum – had abused their children emotionally, physically, and even sexually. Then when the child grew up, he or she heard thoughts in their minds that they thought were their own but were not. The enemy whispered thoughts into their minds such as "Your father did not love you," "You cannot trust your father to protect you," "Your mother wishes you were never born," "Your father hates you," "It is all your fault," "You cannot trust anyone in your life to protect or love you," etc. The enemy whispered these thoughts to them, causing them to believe that the thoughts they were listening to for a lifetime were the truth. Therefore, they began to replay those thoughts in their minds thousands of times, over and over throughout their lives. They began to reason that they could not trust anyone else in their lives and that they must get their own way. Whoever they married would not look out for them nor protect them since their father or mother did not. Therefore, they become controlling and manipulative of their spouse during marriage causing much strife and friction.

The most common marriage in the world today involves one person who is very controlling, demanding and confrontational who marries someone who avoids confrontation and is more submissive. You usually have one who is more of a taker who marries one who is a giver. Thus, they are set up from the start of the marriage for misery, disaster and failure. The hidden spirits within each other are drawing them together and they are completely oblivious to what is actually occurring from the spiritual sense. They look on the outside of each other and if they are attracted to each other at all physically, they'll forget about the enemy spirits within each other until after they are married, and then it is too late. The enemy spirits have succeeded in bringing together two people who are completely unaware of what is about to manifest in the physical. Then they wake up one day and say "Why in the world did I ever fall in love with you, as you have changed and become mean to me!"

People who control other people and would be considered to be type A aggressive are usually operating in a spirit of Jezebel. Those who are more laid back and will not confront others who need to be addressed are usually operating in the Ahab spirit. They are co-dependent on each other and, once married, will have a lifetime of strife due to one person always wanting to enforce their demands over their gentler and giving spouse. If they don't get their way then they will raise their voice, demand and manipulate the other person to do what they want until they give in. The person who is being controlled will ultimately get worn out and feel emasculated from all independent thinking and become disillusioned in life until they feel like they are a puppet on a string. Many put up with this control for years but eventually it wears on them depending on the strength of the Jezebel spirit in their mate. One day they may finally state "enough is enough" and separate or divorce. Or if they really love their spouse they will separate, hoping to get them to change so they can stay married in peace, but usually their spouse will divorce them as they have no more use for them if they cannot control them. They will discard them. Sometimes the controlled victims will start to shut down emotionally and possibly physically, as they will feel like they are dying and becoming a zombie puppet.

These marriages which are wreaked with havoc around the world are being ruined unbeknownst to them by enemy spirits. It is time for everyone in the world to wake up and realize that if you are having challenges in your personal life with relationships, that the enemy is most likely at work behind the scenes. So many couples go to pastors and counselors for help. Unfortunately many pastors and counselors have no idea how the enemy has been speaking to the couples and is the root of their issue. They try to "counsel" the people by telling them to love and respect each other, which is all good, but never gets to the unhealthy root of the situation that is producing unhealthy fruit. Unfortunately, if a Christian or non-believer has an enemy spirit who has a right to them through emotional wounds from their fathers and mothers, then they will not feel plagued. Christians are affected by tormenting enemy spirits all the time. Many of them simply need to be made aware that if they are not living in peace - that the enemy is most likely at work behind the scenes, whispering to them in their thoughts which cause them to lash out at their spouse. They are being told to control and manipulate their spouse and demand that they do something which will cause strife. They simply cannot stop themselves.

I see many in my ministry around the world whose wives or husbands are pastors or leaders in the church, pray in tongues and even operate in prophecy. These people speak very controlling

19

words and take unhealthy actions against their spouses. That is what the spirit of Jezebel does to a person. They literally hear the voice of the enemy in a very strong and real sense which tells them what to do and then they obey the voice and do what they are hearing. The enemy tells them bad things about their spouse and they act upon it. This is the most common reason for strife in marriages and the number one reason for divorce.

Therefore, in order for a person to choose a healthy mate, they must be set free from the enemy having any rights to them, commanding any enemy spirits to go. Then they will be set free from old, unhealthy mindsets before choosing a mate to be married to. Otherwise the person who has the Ahab spirit will unknowingly be drawn to someone with the Jezebel spirit and they will be tormented in strife throughout the marriage. This book was written in order to help people to be freed from the pains of their pasts so they can choose a healthy mate to live with for the rest of their lives. No one wants to have multiple failed marriages or to live in a marriage full of daily misery. There is nothing worse than having your mate despise you and even undermine what you want to accomplish, especially for the Lord. The enemy is always the reason why a marriage or relationship fails.

Most often you have two hurting people who come together hoping to be loved unconditionally by each other, yet both hear the enemy whispering to them in their minds, which cause them to speak words of criticism, harshness or worse. Sometimes you can have one healthy person who marries a very unhealthy person. In those cases the person who is unhealthy will demand their way so many times that it causes their spouse to no longer want to be around them. Then when the spouse pulls away the unhealthy person will be driven by fear to control and force them to stay with them. This never works as the person will pull away on a more permanent basis. Many times the controlling person will want nothing to do with their spouse if they cannot control them any longer.

When people have successfully been delivered from any enemy spirits that have controlled them, they will then be able to make a healthy decision to choose someone who is also healthy. They will live in a marriage where they both want to love on each other unconditionally, the way God intended. The man will love his wife like Christ loved the church, laying his life down. Then the woman will easily submit to his leadership in marriage because he will be directed by God, instead of the enemy or himself. There will be peace in their home and if there are any differences of opinions, they will be discussed in a healthy way instead of through raising one's voice and demanding that they get their way.

So do you want a marriage where you dominate your spouse? I would hope the answer is no. Do you want to be controlled by your spouse on most every decision that needs to be made? Again, I doubt it. You both should want a calm, peaceful and mutually loving relationship to help each other achieve your goals as a couple as well as any individual dreams that you each desire to pursue. It should be a symbiotic relationship in which you want to help each other succeed in your desires of your hearts and for the Lord.

The Lord made a woman to be the helpmate to her husband but unfortunately the women's movement took over trying to replace the husband or to emasculate him of his godly duties. It made the man bow to women and the spirit of Jezebel took over the United States and world. What does it mean to be a helpmate? It means that when the man listens to the Lord for direction that his wife will gladly want to help accomplish what the Lord is directing the man to do. In some relationships the woman hears from the Lord and her husband does not. They are not on the same page spiritually as God intended. So in this case it is simply a fact that the man is not the spiritual leader and he abdicated his responsibility to lead spiritually. Too many men walk around with the spirit of Ahab and need to break free and rise up to be mighty men of valor. My book *Waking The Lion Within: Reclaiming Your Position in Christ* was intended to help men to stand up to be a godly leader in order to lead spiritually in boldness as the Lord intended.

Choosing A Godly Mate will help you look within yourself to make sure you are freed from all generational curses, and enemy spirits in order to be clean and set free. Then and only then should you begin to move forward to choose a healthy mate for yourself, who is also free from any enemy spirits. There is nothing like finding a man or woman to help complete you and live in peace all of your days on earth and work in unity towards the same godly, life goals. Roughly 25% of the couples in the world are able to be free of the enemy and find another healthy mate in order to live in peace and love. I would like to see this percentage increase as much as possible. So many in the church today have marriages that are miserable and all they need to do is look in the mirror at themselves and be honest. Once they admit to some of these unhealthy behaviors and recognize that the enemy is at work within them, then they can successfully get set free once and for all. Then they can make a healthy decision on finding a healthy mate to complete them in Christ. All it takes is an awareness of the truth from within and then to take their authority to command out all enemy spirits that have co-existed in them since a child. It is time to take back what the enemy has stolen and rise up in Christ.

Chapter 1

Is It Good To Be Alone?

Paul said in 1 Corinthians 7:8-9 NKJV, "[8] But I say to the unmarried and to the widows: It is good for them if they remain even as I am; [9] but if they cannot exercise self-control, let them marry. For it is better to marry than to burn with passion." Paul goes on in 1 Corinthians 7:32-33 NKJV, "[32] But I want you to be without care. He who is unmarried cares for the things of the Lord – how he may please the Lord. [33] But he who is married cares about the things of the world – how he may please his wife. [34] There is a difference between a wife and a virgin. The unmarried woman cares about the things of the Lord, that she may be holy both in body and in spirit. But she who is married cares about the things of the world – how she may please her husband. [35] And this I say for your own profit, not that I may put a leash on you, but for what is proper, and that you may serve the Lord without distraction. [36] But if any man thinks he is behaving improperly toward his virgin, if she is past the flower of youth, and thus it must be, let him do what he wishes. He does not sin; let them marry. [37] Nevertheless he who stands steadfast in his heart, having no necessity, but has power over his own will, and has so determined in his heart that he will keep his virgin, does well. [38] So then he who gives her in marriage does well, but he who does not give her in marriage does better."

I can speak to what Paul is saying first hand. I have been married twice. With my first wife I had no desires to pursue full time ministry as I simply wanted to work in corporate America, making as much money as I could to enjoy the finer things in life. I was like most people in the United States who wanted to live in a nice home, drive newer cars, have three children, go to a nice large church where other people who were successful in business went and then when the end of my life came I hoped I would make it to heaven. But then after I went through a divorce that I did not want, in part due to stress from a child who was out of control, the Lord then got ahold of me and radically changed my heart. I no longer was interested in pursuing the almighty dollar but wanted to help people get set free from the enemy due to my own personal experiences of how the enemy affected my family.

During my second marriage my wife was tormented strongly by the spirit of Jezebel and Leviathan, causing her to control, manipulate and abuse me at a very extreme level. The Lord wanted me to marry her so that after six years of tribulation I would learn the tactics of the enemy at an intimate and extreme level in order to ultimately come out of it with an extreme anointing to help millions around the world to get set free from those spirits. I had to endure one of the most extreme cases because of some people I would eventually minister to who also endured a similar tribulation. To receive one of the most extreme anointings for delivering one of the most extreme enemy spirits, one must endure one of the most extreme tribulations. In other words, the more extreme your personal

24

sacrifice in life, the more extreme your anointing for helping others can be once you are healed and come out the other side.

I learned so much during those six years about exactly how the enemy worked and why a person develops it (due to father and mother wounds as a child). She ultimately tried to stop me from doing what the Lord wanted both of us to do in ministry. The Lord wanted us to help other hurting couples to get set free from controlling spirits, heal the sick and prophesy words from the Lord to help guide people into their destinies. So the Lord finally released me to separate from my wife - as the spirits in her wanted to shut my ministry completely down, which is exactly what Jezebel tried doing to Elijah in the Old Testament in 1 and 2 Kings.

So when the Lord finally told me to separate on January 23, 2015, He began to set up His ministry through me and told me it would grow rapidly around the world. Unfortunately my wife did not want to admit to her behavior and lied about me to people in our church, family and friends, instead of telling the truth and getting set free. The Lord told me that people who knew us would eventually not believe the lies she told about me because they would see the fruit of my ministry growing rapidly to accomplish what His directives were. Within months I started to get people set free from the spirits of Jezebel, Leviathan and Ahab and saw their lives changed radically and marriages saved. I was no longer being stopped by my spouse to do exactly what the Lord directed me to do. The ministry grew quickly as people came from around the world through Facebook, Skype, FaceTime and my website www.restoredtofreedom.com as the doors opened up everywhere. I was finally able to do everything the Lord wanted me to accomplish as my interests were no longer divided and Jezebel could not stop what the Lord wanted to see come to pass.

The Lord had me write my first book, *Restored to Freedom,* which came out in March of 2016. People around the world began to finally have the revelation of what I had learned, how father wounds (and strong mother wounds) could cause the spirit of Jezebel and

Leviathan to gain access to people (many in the church) and cause them to control and manipulate others. Then the Lord had me write five more books in the next twelve months to help people get set freed from the Ahab spirit, learn about their authority in Christ, love hard to love people like Christ loved the church, walk in more peace and have a higher level of faith. I did thousands of individual private deliverance sessions over Facebook Messenger with people from New Zealand, Australia, South Africa, England, Ireland, Scotland, Pakistan, India, and most every state in the U.S. and Canada. The Lord started promoting me on Christian TV stations, radio, internet shows and then told me in February to start doing Worldwide Deliverance Sessions using Facebook LIVE. In March of 2017, on my first Worldwide Deliverance Session, I saw 2,000 people who joined the broadcast live and then over 11,000 watched the same broadcast session within a few weeks as more shared it. Thousands were getting delivered and healed, saving their marriages and increasing their anointings and giftings in ministry from the Lord. By the summer of 2017 there were thousands that were being delivered around the world through monthly Worldwide Deliverance Sessions on Facebook LIVE.

Although I informed my wife what she had been battling for a lifetime, she refused to get delivered and instead chose to keep the spirits in her. Without a wife being affected by Jezebel and Leviathan to cause me to have my interests divided, I was able to do exactly what the Lord asked me to do and before I knew it I had one of the busiest Healing Rooms in the United States with people coming from multiple states around the country to get delivered from enemy spirits and healed from physical sickness and disease.

Near the end of 2016 the Lord had me start speaking in various cities around the country and staying for a week, two weeks and sometimes three or more weeks to minister in various regions and states around the United States. The Lord had me travel at a moment's notice as I drove to most of the places, keeping my books inside my vehicle. In April of 2017 I flew to California and stayed in people's homes for three weeks and did a lot of corporate deliverance / healing sessions and Healing Room trainings, but also did a lot of personal sessions helping people get set free. Then in June of 2017 I traveled to New York City, New Jersey, Virginia, Pennsylvania, Ohio, Texas, North Carolina, and Tennessee, as the demand from people for freedom grew rapidly. In July I went to Sandusky, Ohio and then Houston and College Station, Texas. In August I traveled to Buffalo, Rochester, Little Valley, and Jamestown, New York and then Campbellsville, Kentucky. In September I returned to Houston, and College Station, Texas and then traveled to Bethlehem, Pennsylvania with plans to visit Reno, Nevada and a Paiute Indian reservation before returning back to Houston, Texas in late October.

The point of all of this is to show how the Lord was able to accomplish what He needed far quicker with me being single and focused instead of married with my attention divided. Will He eventually connect me with a healthy wife - free from Jezebel (but having extensive experience with dealing with Jezebel / Leviathan and Ahab) in the future? Absolutely! But not until I have completed setting up the first phase of the Lord's plan. In September of 2017 the Lord connected me with the Kingdom Broadcasting Network in Houston, Texas to start my first TV show, aptly named Restored To Freedom. This was right after Houston suffered from the worst disasters in history with Hurricane Harvey. The TV show focuses on getting people aware of the enemy spirits and then helping them get set free. God is on the move and wants His people to be freed from the enemy and operating in the fullness of their callings and increasing their anointings.

Do most single people desire to have their own full time ministries? No, but there are many who desire to be married to people who are godly, attending church and some desire to marry someone in a full time ministry. It is very important for those who already have their own ministries or desire to do more in ministry to be extremely discerning of who they marry, so as not to marry someone who has a controlling spirit of Jezebel which would want to cause confusion and shut them down. Jezebel always will draw to those either in ministry or in a church so as to create strife and confusion. Therefore, it is so important for every pastor in the world to be freed from the Ahab and Jezebel spirit so they can address it within their church.

One pastor from Indiana shared with me that over 50% of the pastors and over 70% of men in America suffer from looking at pornography. The Lord showed me that those who suffer from pornography largely also have the spirit of Ahab on them. That is why so many pastors are not able to speak to being pure and righteous in the Lord and being freed from spirits because they are feeling condemned by the enemy because they are guilty themselves. So many pastors have the Ahab spirit and allow those in leadership around them to operate in the Jezebel spirit, who then control the church. It is time for all pastors in the world to get set free from Ahab and Jezebel and become a mighty man of valor, pure and righteous before the Lord and preach the whole truth in the Bible. They need to be pure and righteous so the church will flourish. God is exposing this around the world like never before. A pastor in Ohio was dealing with a wife who operated in the Jezebel spirit. He finally had enough of the torment and called his elders and leaders of the church together to address his wife. She denied she had it and chose to keep the spirit of Jezebel and decided to leave that church. A month later she died from hemorrhaging from her mouth. She was 32 years of age. God is very serious about getting people to tell the truth and getting freed.

Revelation 2:19-23 NKJV states, "[19] I know your works, love, service, faith, and your patience; and as for your works, the last are more than the first. [20] Nevertheless I have a few things against you, because you allow that woman Jezebel, who calls herself a prophetess, to teach and seduce My servants to commit sexual immorality and eat things sacrificed to idols. [21] And I gave her time to repent of her sexual immorality, and she did not repent. [22] Indeed I will cast her into a sickbed, and those who commit adultery with her into great tribulation, unless they repent of their deeds. [23] I will kill her children with death, and all the churches shall know that I am He who searches the minds and hearts. And I will give to each one of you according to your works."

God is cleaning up His church and if you are operating in that spirit and choose not to admit it and get delivered then you could die. A woman from New Zealand denied she had it in front of her family who confronted her. She took two steps to walk away and then died instantly.

Stating all of this, most people in the world want to be married. Some desire marriage due to their fleshly desires to have a sexual relationship that is blessed by the Lord. Others do not want to be alone due to fear or having no one to talk to in the evenings. I have a new appreciation and respect for single, attractive women who have either gone through divorces or are simply single by choice. I personally know many who are being pursued by so-called "Christian" men who want to have lustful, sexual relations with them before marriage. It is an abomination to the Lord and makes me personally angry and disgusted. I even know of some pastors who have pursued attractive women on Facebook and Instagram and sent them suggestive photos and videos of themselves or other women trying to lure them in. God knows and sees all and your lives and ministries will be exposed and shut down if you do not repent before God and turn from your wicked and perverse ways.

If you are a woman who likes attention from men who are not godly and pursue them back, then you are playing with fire and could be burned as well. You are to have nothing to do with anyone who you know who has a sexual perverse spirit in them and is communicating to you and should block them completely on social media and your life. Too many love the attention they receive and the enemy knows it. The more pictures they post of themselves the more LIKES they get on Facebook and the more comments they receive which feed their fleshly desires to want to feel wanted and loved. Unfortunately many get burned because they waste valuable time messaging men who are not godly whatsoever. You cannot flirt with the enemy and be unscathed. Rise up to be a Proverbs 31 woman – reprinted below is Proverbs 31 10-31 NKJV:

The Virtuous Wife

10 Who can find a virtuous wife?
For her worth is far above rubies.

11 The heart of her husband safely trusts her;
So he will have no lack of gain.

12 She does him good and not evil
All the days of her life.

13 She seeks wool and flax,
And willingly works with her hands.

14 She is like the merchant ships,
She brings her food from afar.

15 She also rises while it is yet night,
And provides food for her household,
And a portion for her maidservants.

16 She considers a field and buys it;
From her profits she plants a vineyard.

17 She girds herself with strength,
And strengthens her arms.

18 She perceives that her merchandise is good,
And her lamp does not go out by night.

19 She stretches out her hands to the distaff,
And her hand holds the spindle.

20 She extends her hand to the poor,
Yes, she reaches out her hands to the needy.

21 She is not afraid of snow for her household,
For all her household is clothed with scarlet.

22 She makes tapestry for herself;
Her clothing is fine linen and purple.

23 Her husband is known in the gates,
When he sits among the elders of the land.

24 She makes linen garments and sells them,
And supplies sashes for the merchants.

25 Strength and honor are her clothing;
She shall rejoice in time to come.

26 She opens her mouth with wisdom,
And on her tongue is the law of kindness.

27 She watches over the ways of her household,
And does not eat the bread of idleness.

28 Her children rise up and call her blessed;
Her husband also, and he praises her:

29 "Many daughters have done well,
But you excel them all."

30 Charm is deceitful and beauty is passing,
But a woman who fears the Lord, she shall be praised.

31 Give her of the fruit of her hands,
And let her own works praise her in the gates.

Many women have unfortunately decided to get married to a man because they "feel" emotionally attached to someone who is unhealthy or they are growing older and are tired of being alone so will settle for someone less than godly. Then they ignore all of the "red flags" and checks in their spirits. Many men desire to get married so they can have sex - plain and simple and very fleshly. But many men who are operating in the spirit of Ahab, unwittingly choose an attractive woman from the physical appearance and then ignore what is inside of the woman's heart (much pain from feeling ignored, rejected or controlled by their fathers). Then after they get married they discover that their wife is very controlling, manipulative and verbally abusive and thus causes them to wish they were single and in peace again. Of course, women can also choose men who are very controlling and abusive and then they set themselves up for disaster as their bodies cannot take constant verbal abuse over and over for years.

So what are some of the unhealthy reasons to be married to someone?

- Feeling lonely.
- Desperate for companionship.
- Desire for sex.
- Have financial needs that you want paid off.
- Desire a father or mother for your children.
- You feel depressed / sad most of the time.
- You live in fear / anxiety most of the time.
- You want someone to care for you.

- You are a Christian and are willing to marry someone who is physically attractive or wealthy but is not truly godly.

So what are some of the healthier reasons to be married to someone?
- Desire to love someone unconditionally as Christ loved the church and you are willing to lay your life down for them.
- You want to love your spouse more than you need them to love you. You have so much love that you want to give to another person.
- You have been healed of all past wounds from childhood and other broken relationships and are now ready to love a person as Christ would have you.
- To accomplish a mutual life goal or purpose with each other such as helping people who are hurting, loving on children, a joint ministry that each other has desires for together. If you have a mutual goal that you both share then you will be more likely to spend more time together serving. Most people do not have mutual life goals that they share together and thus drift apart.
- A healthy compliment to each other's strengths / weaknesses as long as they are not totally out of line with your Christian walk. One may be strong administratively and the other is more "big picture" focused. One may be gifted in writing while the other loves to speak in front of groups or in the media. You compliment each other well.
- You each have similar desires / activities that you would enjoy pursuing together (both workout / eat same type of food / reading / travel / ministry, etc.)
- Have similar sense of playful humor so you both bring life to each other as well as other people. It is important to laugh and enjoy life because if you get married to a

33

person who is serious all the time or negative when you are upbeat and positive, then you will be frustrated and discouraged.

It is very important that when you decide to marry another person that you both have similar goals and understand them up front and not after you are married. Have you ever really thought about why you want to be married? If it is just because you are lonely and want to have sex with someone then that will fade away within a few months of the wedding night as you get to know the real person inside of them. You need to go deeper and see if the two of you are truly aligned for success in the long term and also from a spiritual aspect. Obviously if one person has a strong interest in doing full time ministry and serving the Lord and the other just wants to work in the corporate world then their interests will be divided and they both will be miserable and frustrated in living single lives within marriage. If one person is very educated and the other is not, then they will not have anything to talk about that will stimulate each other because the higher educated one will want to talk about things that the spouse will have no understanding of.

So the answer to the question "is it good to be alone?" is yes and no. It is good to be alone until you have healed from all of your wounds from your past because if not, you will have pain that you will take out on your spouse due to hearing the voices of the enemy within you. You will have spirits that will be whispering to you, causing you not to love your spouse unconditionally. The spirits of Jezebel / Leviathan and Ahab will have a legal right to you until you recognize it and take authority. If you have been set free from the pain from your past and commanded the enemy spirits to go - then you are ready to love someone with all of your heart.

The Lord may want you to remain single for a season in order to accomplish a ministry being birthed and then eventually He can bring you the love of your life who also is being worked on to completion by the Lord. You need to truly listen and be directed by the Lord and He will confirm along the way. It is so important that both people hear from the Lord independently and are not influenced through manipulative and coercive comments and behaviors by your mate.

Assuming you have been healed and delivered, then the answer is that you are ready to be married if you desire, but you need to be careful and choose a spouse that will also be healthy from their own soul wounds from their pasts and delivered from any enemy spirits. So many people will act like they are everything that you want them to be at first if they find you attractive. They may even check out your Facebook, Instagram and other social media pages to see what you post about and like in order to mirror that. They want to become who they think you want them to be so that they can get you. But as soon as they think they have you, they will eventually pull off their deceptive mask and switch back to who they really are and then you will be disillusioned, shocked and hurt.

The purpose of this book is to help you discern who to marry who is healthy but also to make sure you are healthy in order to make a wise choice of who to marry. If you are both hurting and are not set free from any enemy spirits, which most people are, then you will both hurt worse when married as the enemy will come out in both of you against each other and words will be spoken that will hurt each of you more deeply. There is nothing like it in the world to be married to a person who loves you unconditionally with all of their heart. But conversely there is nothing worse to be married to someone who wants to control, manipulate and make you do what they want out of the pain that they suffered in their lives as a child. Being controlled and forced to do what the enemy wants them to do will be far worse than any stint of living in solitary confinement, yet in peace.

In other words, before you decide to get married, make sure that you are in a healthy place with which to make the decision to date and choose a life partner. Then you can marry with more discernment on the front end of your decisioning process. You do not want to marry because you feel lonely, desperate for companionship and wanting sex. You need to be content, at peace and enjoying your life of singleness and then you can discern who to conjoin yourself to later in marriage. Marriage should be a lifetime commitment because once you have gone through one divorce, you are more likely to keep divorcing as it becomes easier as you keep your demons from your past and they keep drawing you to another person who has demons that you both become co-dependent on. Jezebels attract Ahabs and Ahabs attract Jezebels. It's time to be set free forever from the enemy's legal rights to control you so that you can choose a healthy mate from the Lord. When the clouds from the enemy have been blown from your eyes and you can discern clearly about a potential mate, then you will be able to see who they really are and they cannot hide from you the person who lurks inside of them. Then you will not have to worry that you are picking someone who will change into someone that wants to torment you for a lifetime. God wants your eyes to be wide open so you can make the wisest choice possible.

Chapter 2

Our Pasts Control Our Future

When young people decide that they want to be married they do not often think anything about how their pasts will affect their future. They fall "in love" with a person and allow their emotions to drive their desires and before they know it they are making life-affecting decisions based upon a few months or year or two of "dating" when people try to put on a front of who they believe the other person wants them to be. They feel "in love" and totally throw out the window all common sense and any possible hint of spiritual discernment. They let their eyes focus on their mate's hair, eyes, body, humor, and totally ignore their heart and who they actually are behind closed doors. They do not see inside their spirit as to whom they are when no one is looking but God.

What people do not think about is what happens when a person grows up in a family that has little to no unconditional love and how it may affect a young woman or man for the rest of their lives. I know that I never thought about it as I grew up in a home where I was loved by both of my parents as that was my "normal" and thought most everyone else had a similar "normal." But so many grow up with either one parent or both who were not involved in their life. They may even have felt rejected, criticized, controlled or hurt in extreme ways by them. Some may have even been abused verbally, physically or sexually. So what exactly happens when a child grows up with the lack of unconditional love or rejection from a parent? They begin to hear the enemy whispering to them in their mind and think that what they are hearing is just their own thoughts. The enemy tells them that they are not loved by one parent or both. They feel like they have to be perfect to earn just a little bit of love from one parent or both. In some cases they cannot do anything to earn their love, and thus they believe that they cannot trust anyone else to love them. They have a lot of fear, anxiety and pain which drives them to control other people, making their lives miserable. The enemy continues to whisper to them, which drives them to force others to do exactly what they want and it ultimately drives a huge wedge between them and their spouse and other relationships (work, church, sports, etc). They often will be involved in multiple broken relationships, divorces, anger, pain, sadness and depression.

They are unknowingly operating in the spirit of Jezebel which causes people to control, manipulate, lie, and have selfish sexual desires to either want sex all the time or use it to limit their partner to control them to do exactly what they want.

So just who was Jezebel in the Old Testament? It is important to know the history of the woman that took on the moniker for these insidious behaviors.

Scripture References—1 Kings 16:31; 18:4-19; 19:1, 2; 21:5-25; 2 Kings 9

The spirits of control, manipulation, deceit, seduction, witchcraft and murder which came against God's anointed were operating in the world long before the woman who exemplified these spirits was born. Queen Jezebel symbolized the combined capabilities of all these spirits better than anyone and thus naming this spirit after her was most appropriate. Bible Gateway does a great job of explaining more in detail about the woman of Jezebel. This scheming and evil woman with a history of murder truly represented the spirit that bore her name as by nature she was a most proud, immoral, manipulative and even murderous woman. She was a seductress, using all the ploys of a sensual woman trying to lure in her prey using all her methods both physically and emotionally. Jezebel was rejected by her father and had a controlling mother.

She was the daughter of Ethbaal, king of the Zidonians, and priest of Baal worshipers. The Phoenicians were an extraordinary race, and outstanding as the great sea faring peoples of the ancient world, but they were idolaters who regarded God as only a local deity, "the god of the land." Their gods were Baal and Ashtaroth or Astarte, with their innumerable number of priests, 450 of whom Ahab used in the amazing temple to the Sun-god he had built in Samaria. Another 400 priests were housed in a sanctuary that Jezebel built for them, and whom she provided food from her own table. Perverse and evil rites were associated with the worship of Baal including child sacrifice.

It was this ungodly woman who married Ahab who was the king of Northern Israel, and who in so doing was guilty of a rash and damaging act which resulted in evil consequences. As a Jew, Ahab sinned against his own Hebrew faith by taking as his wife the daughter of a man whose very name, Ethbaal, meant, "A Man of Baal." Ahab was captivated by her beauty and commanding character and fell for her, and Jezebel, cunning and proud, eagerly seized the opportunity of sharing the throne of a king.

Any man, able to resist the wiles of a beautiful but wicked woman possesses true heroism. Joseph succeeded against the lovely yet lustful wife of Potiphar, but Caesar and Antony after conquering almost the whole world, were conquered by Cleopatra. Ahab, enchanted by Jezebel, took her to be his wife, and served Baal and worshipped him. All the other sins of Ahab were minor as compared to his marriage to Jezebel and serving Baal that followed. 1 Kings 16:30-32 NKJV states, *"30 Now Ahab the son of Omri did evil in the sight of the Lord, more than all who were before him. 31 And it came to pass, as though it had been an insignificant thing for him to walk in the sins of Jeroboam the son of Nebat that he took as wife Jezebel the daughter of Ethbaal, king of the Sidonians and he went and served Baal and worshiped him. 32 Then he set up an altar for Baal in the temple of Baal, which he had built in Samaria."* For over 60 years idolatry had made a horrible life for the Hebrews and meant more to them than the breaking of the first two commandments of the law; it produced spiritual and moral disintegration which was intensified by Jezebel's determined effort to destroy the worship of the one and true God. What was the character of Jezebel? Her name has become a prominent cliché for seductive power, worldly subtlety and evil of the worst type throughout the ages.

Jezebel was no ordinary woman who was misguided through an error in judgment. Her behavior caused her to attract the immediate attention of all that came into her presence. Though by no means a sweet and loving person, she had a masculine and militaristic demand of others, and was dominated by her extraordinary force of character. Jezebel's life came to an awful fate with a just ending which belongs to no other woman of the Bible. While the Bible does not go into great detail about her character, it simply sets forth the events in which she bore such a major part, yet as we read between the lines we see her as a woman of powerful force, intellect, and will. She knew nothing of the restraint of higher pure principles. Savage and relentless, this proud and strong-minded woman carried out her foul schemes and whoever got in her way would face a terrible ending. A skillful woman, she prostituted all her gifts for the continuance of evil, and her misused talents became a curse. Persuasive, her influence was wrongly directed. Nothing would or could stop her in the flesh. Unyielding above other women, she used her strength of character to destroy a king and her own descendants, as well as corrupt the life of an entire nation.

Baal had no more devoted follower than Jezebel. None could match her desire for the worship of Ashtaroth the famous goddess of the Zidonians, as zealous and liberal maintenance of hundreds of idolatrous priests clearly proves. Not content with establishing the idol worship of her own country in her husband's court, she desired to convert the entire nation of Israel to Baal worship. Two heathen sanctuaries were built, one at Samaria with its 450 priests, and the other at Jezreel with its 400 priests. In a most relentless fashion Jezebel tried to drive out the true prophets of God from the land, and thus became the first religious female persecutor in history by using the power that was given to her by her husband King Ahab. From her idolatrous father, a high priest of Ashtaroth, she inherited her fanatical religious enthusiasm which inspired her to exterminate the worship of the true and living God, and almost succeeded in the attempt.

The overtaking of the nation with all the sins and cruel superstitions of such a discouraging cult as Baalism brought upon the scene the chief of the true prophets, Elijah. He appeared suddenly before Ahab, predicted three years of drought, and at the end of the period unexpectedly appeared again and challenged the 850 prophets of Baal to a supreme test of power. The confrontation took place at the top of Mount Carmel which today overlooks the valley of Megiddo which is to be the place of the final battle of Armageddon that will take place during the end times before the second coming of Christ. Elijah taunted them making fun of their gods for sleeping and then with great boldness commanded fire to fall from heaven and then took back the control from Jezebel and had the people kill all the priests of Baal while Ahab escaped back home to Jezebel to report on what happened.

After such an overwhelming victory, once Elijah heard about Jezebel's threat (which is a very common ploy to be threatened by people who host the Jezebel spirit which cause fear in their victims) to kill Elijah and his partners "by tomorrow at this time" caused him to fear and he felt that the fury of a murderous woman was more than he could face. The spirit of controlling fear caused him to flee for his life across the kingdom of Judah, leaving the arrogant queen, for the time being, in undeniable possession of the land.

Ahab was like a puppet in the hands of his overpowering wife. He was compliant and weak which made it easy for Jezebel to achieve her murderous designs. How could worthless and spineless Ahab resist the evil scheming of his immoral partner? It was Jezebel who became feared commander in Israel and not the cowardly husband she could put under her thumb. Ahab was more luxury-loving and sensual than cruel, but under the complete domination of a ruthless woman he was forced to act against his finer feelings. Without Ahab's authority, Jezebel would have been a serpent without fangs. In this marriage, Ahab was the weaker vessel with a wife who mocked his diligent scruples and bound him in all wickedness as with strong chains.

Our Lord used a striking figure to illustrate the continuing influence of evil, emanating from a life devoid of godly principles—

Do men gather grapes of thorns, or figs of thistles? .... a corrupt tree brings forth evil fruit .... a corrupt tree cannot bring forth good fruit (Matthew 7:16-20).

Jezebel had a rotten root and so everything connected with her was contaminated. With her strength of character, lust for power, remorseless rejection of godliness, and unshrinking and resolute activity to eliminate all that interferes with the satisfaction of her wicked designs, she was evil in every imaginable way.

Her children continued in the wickedness in which they were raised. Jezebel's evil influence was revived in her daughter Athaliah of Judea. Her maligned character reappears in her eldest son, Ahaziah, who, like his idolatrous mother, was a devout worshiper of Baal. Her second son, Jehoram or Joram, was another image of his mother—further corrupt fruit from a corrupt tree. It was Jehoram, who heard from the lips of Jehu who had been raised up to obliterate the Ahab dynasty, that there would be no peace in Israel, "so long as the whoredoms of thy mother Jezebel and her witchcrafts are so many" (2 Kings 9:22). Is it to be pondered that Jehoram suffered a similar fate to that of his mother's at the hands of Jehu?

The tragedy of Naboth and his vineyard reveals how vicious a woman Jezebel was. Life was cheap to such a female who had murder in her veins. Her father, Ethbaal, murdered his predecessor, Phelles. Brought up in such a home of intrigue and murder, what else could we expect but a she-devil as Jezebel had become?

Naboth's refusal was the introduction to one of the strangest, most powerful, and most terrible stories of the Bible; a drama, on the one side, of innocence, courage, independence, and the fear of God, and, on the other side, of covetousness, greediness, cruelty, perjury, death and terrible revenge.

Jezebel was prepared to murder in her stride toward the desired objective, as the incident of Naboth's vineyard reveals. King Ahab happened to see this fruitful vineyard and inquired as to its owner. Learning it belonged to Naboth; Ahab called him to the palace and offered to buy the vineyard. But it was not for sale. It had belonged to his forefathers and had become precious to Naboth, and as an Israelite Ahab understood his desire to retain it. Thwarted in what he coveted, Ahab took to his bed and fasted.

Jezebel came upon the scene. Learning what had happened, and, as a foreigner from a country where the wishes of a king were never questioned, she revealed herself as a woman of accumulated authority when she consoled Ahab by saying—

"Arise and eat bread, and let thine heart be merry. I will give thee the vineyard of Naboth the Jezreelite."

Jezebel ordered, by letter, stamped with the royal seal, a public feast. She also instituted an assembly of the people of Jezreel to try the pure and Godly Naboth for blasphemies against God and the king. Naboth was arrested, tried and convicted on the accounts of false witnesses secured by Jezebel. She found these witnesses in order to appear within the bounds of the law. Found guilty, Naboth was stoned until his innocent life was crushed out of him. Ahab took possession of the much-coveted vineyard. But the blood of godly Naboth did not cry out in vain. God called Elijah out of his retirement to go to Ahab and pronounce the fearful doom awaiting the murderous pair and their unholy seed. The prophet told the king of his fate—

"In the place where the dogs licked the blood of Naboth, shall dogs lick thy blood, even thine."

This prophecy was fulfilled shortly after its pronouncement for war broke out between the Israelites and the Syrians, and Ahab, while riding in his chariot, received his death wound. The blood-soaked chariot was taken to the spring which ran through Naboth's vineyard, and the dogs came and licked up the bloody water. Concerning Jezebel, Elijah said, "The dogs shall eat Jezebel by the wall of Jezreel," and shortly we shall see how this prophecy was also fulfilled to the very letter.

The death of Ahab, the one whom Jezebel had "stirred up to work wickedness in the sight of the Lord" revealed her to be proud and unable to have any feelings of repentance. There was no sign of sorrow in her, as she went out proudly to meet her prophesied doom. Jehu had been appointed and anointed as the avenger of God, and he set about his grim task of dealing out justice to those who had polluted the land. Jezebel's son and grandson met Jehu in the blood-stained vineyard Naboth had once possessed. Jehu killed Jezebel's son, the king of Israel, and her grandson was overtaken while trying to get away and was killed. The still proud, defiant queen-mother knew her last hour was not far away, and great-grandmother though she was, she took time to arrange her hair and paint her face, and looked out at a window to greet Jehu as he passed by. Jezebel did not paint her face from any motive of vanity because she knew that death was ready to finally take her. Therefore, she determined to die like a queen....so Jezebel painted her eyes and placed her jeweled crown upon her head; then, mounting to the palace tower, she watched the impressive advance of Jehu's chariot.

One item in her sinful life that gave rise to the bitter taunt, "a painted Jezebel," as painting the face was accepted as evidence that a woman had loose morals. Certainly no woman's name in history has become as commonly accepted as a symbol for wickedness.

The climax came as Jehu entered the city gate. Reaching the palace, he looked up to the window from which came the taunting voice of Jezebel: "Is it peace, thou Zimri, thou murderer of thy master?" Such a taunt angered her triumphant enemy, and seeing the two eunuchs standing at the window with the defiant queen he shouted up to them, "Who is on my side? Who? Throw her down!"

They obeyed and threw her out of the window, and as she fell the walls were sprinkled with her blood. Below her were the soldiers with their spears, the horses to tread her underfoot and the hungry dogs waiting for her flesh. The triumphant Jehu entered the palace over Jezebel's dead body. As he ate and drank where she was just standing, he remembered that the one who had just died as prophesied had been a queen and a mother of kings, so he ordered—

"Go, see now this cursed woman, and bury her. And they went to bury her, but they found no more of her than the skull, and the feet, and the palms of her hands."

So Jezebel perished, the idolater, the tyrant, the murderess. She had sown to the wind, and reaped the whirlwind. Many of the godly in Israel must have felt that while Jezebel held evil influence over the land, the deliverance by God seemed to come slowly. But

God's retribution eventually did come. Thus Jezebel encountered a "mysterious, terrible and divine reckoning."

As we turn from our picture of one of the most wicked women who ever breathed, there are one or two lessons to learn from her deeply tainted record. No matter from what angle we approach the life of Jezebel, she stands out as an example to both nations and individuals that the wages of sin is truly death. Further, from this great tragic figure of the Bible we learn how important it is for the influence of a wife and mother to be on the side of all that is good and noble. As Ahab's evil genius, Jezebel was the absolute denial of all God meant a woman to be, namely, a true help-mate of man who was loving and nurturing and supportive. Ahab, as we read, was "stirred up" by Jezebel but stirred up in the wrong direction. When a man marries a woman because of her beauty or forceful personality, or marries a wicked woman or one opposed to his religion, he usually brings sorrow, heartache and disappointment. Jezebel retained her obstinate, inflexible character to the very end. The death of the man whose life she contaminated brought no repentance. What a different story could have been written if only she had learned how to stir up her husband and children to love God and follow good works (2 Timothy 1:6; 2 Peter 1:13). Her misdirected talents, however, brought upon her a curse. The evil she perpetrated was done under the guise of religion.

Finally, evil, witchcraft, and godlessness bring their own reward, and the wicked reap what they sow. Justice overtook Jezebel when her body was thrown out of the window to be torn and mangled, and then eaten by dogs. As a daughter of the devil, she suffers a worse retribution in the realms of the doomed.

There are those who reject such a lurid description of the fate of the wicked who, like Jezebel, defy and deny God, but the divine Word still stands, that Christ is to be revealed from heaven to take vengeance on those who spurn God and who reject the saving Gospel of His beloved Son.

46

2 Thessalonians 1:5-10 NKJV "*5 which is manifest evidence of the righteous judgment of God, that you may be counted worthy of the kingdom of God, for which you also suffer; 6 since it is a righteous thing with God to repay with tribulation those who trouble you,7 and to give you who are troubled rest with us when the Lord Jesus is revealed from heaven with His mighty angels, 8 in flaming fire taking vengeance on those who do not obey the gospel of our Lord Jesus Christ. 9 These shall be punished with everlasting destruction from the presence of the Lord and from the Glory of His power, 10 when He comes, in that Day, to be glorified in His saints and to be admired among all those who believe, because our testimony among you was believed."*

Several have asked the question....can a person truly host all that is a part of the Jezebel spirit and be a pure and loving Christian at the same time? Although they are able to hear from the Lord at times and even give prophetic words that are right on – they also hear from the enemy spirit often which causes them to behave contrary to the Holy Spirit. Thus they behave like a Dr. Jekyll and Mr. Hyde to their spouse and children and potentially other victims. It is truly a tormented state for them and their loved ones to live in. If you have a strong gift of discernment in the spirit you can see when the spirit of Jezebel is on an individual as their face looks fake and deceptive and they will overact like they are loving and sweet while being put off by people that they believe are beneath them. There will be times though when the person feels convicted by being around a person who is strong in the Lord and can see through them into their spirit that the person will break down in tears and know that the person knows the truth about them. That is the real person that is then coming through of who they are without the spirit affecting them. Often times you may only see the real side of who they are in Christ just 25% of the time. Sometimes if they are not as affected by Jezebel you may see it 50-75% of the time. The point is to be discerning and wise and truly help them to be able to see the

Jezebel spirit influence in their lives and bring it to their attention in a loving and gentle way so they can get total freedom from their life of deception, lies and torment.

People who operate out of the spirit of Jezebel will also operate in the spirit of Leviathan (Job 41), which causes them to have a strong spirit of pride and twist the truth in their minds.

Leviathan is depicted as having seven heads which are Pride, A Critical Spirit, Confusion (Stupor), Impatience, A Lying tongue (Deception) and Contention (Discord, Hate, Murder). These are reflected in Proverbs 6:16-19: NKJV *"These six things the Lord hates, Yes, seven are an abomination to Him: A proud look, A lying tongue, Hands that shed innocent blood, A heart that devises wicked plans, Feet that are swift in running to evil, A false witness who speaks lies, And one who sows discord among brethren."*

Below is Job 41 which describes the Leviathan spirit:
New King James Version (NKJV)

1 "Can you draw out Leviathan with a hook,
   Or snare his tongue with a line which you lower?

2 Can you put a reed through his nose,
   Or pierce his jaw with a hook?

3 Will he make many supplications to you?
   Will he speak softly to you?

4 Will he make a covenant with you?
   Will you take him as a servant forever?

5 Will you play with him as with a bird,
   Or will you leash him for your maidens?

6 Will your companions make a banquet of him?
  Will they apportion him among the merchants?

7 Can you fill his skin with harpoons,
  Or his head with fishing spears?

8 Lay your hand on him;
  Remember the battle—
  Never do it again!

9 Indeed, any hope of overcoming him is false;
  Shall one not be overwhelmed at the sight of him?

10 No one is so fierce that he would dare stir him up.
  Who then is able to stand against Me?

11 Who has preceded Me, that I should pay him?
  Everything under heaven is Mine.

12 "I will not conceal his limbs,
  His mighty power, or his graceful proportions.

13 Who can remove his outer coat?
  Who can approach him with a double bridle?

14 Who can open the doors of his face,
  With his terrible teeth all around?

15 His rows of scales are his pride,
  Shut up tightly as with a seal;

16 One is so near another
  That no air can come between them;

17 They are joined one to another,
  They stick together and cannot be parted.

18 His sneezings flash forth light,
  And his eyes are like the eyelids of the morning.

19 Out of his mouth go burning lights;
  Sparks of fire shoot out.

20 Smoke goes out of his nostrils,
  As from a boiling pot and burning rushes.

21 His breath kindles coals,
  And a flame goes out of his mouth.

22 Strength dwells in his neck,
  And sorrow dances before him.

23 The folds of his flesh are joined together;
  They are firm on him and cannot be moved.

24 His heart is as hard as stone,
  Even as hard as the lower millstone.

25 When he raises himself up, the mighty are afraid;
   Because of his crashings they are beside themselves.

26 Though the sword reaches him, it cannot avail;
   Nor does spear, dart, or javelin.

27 He regards iron as straw,
   And bronze as rotten wood.

28 The arrow cannot make him flee;
   Slingstones become like stubble to him.

29 Darts are regarded as straw;
   He laughs at the threat of javelins.

30 His undersides are like sharp potsherds;
   He spreads pointed marks in the mire.

31 He makes the deep boil like a pot;
   He makes the sea like a pot of ointment.

32 He leaves a shining wake behind him;
   One would think the deep had white hair.

33 On earth there is nothing like him,
   Which is made without fear.

34 He beholds every high thing;
   He is king over all the children of pride.

Leviathan causes a lot of physical pain and sickness in the body including back and neck pain, insomnia, causes you to fall asleep when trying to read the Word or listen to someone preach a message and can even cause headaches, Fibromyalgia and cancer. Jezebel and Leviathan are the number one reason for strife in a marriage and for divorces that ensue. I can confirm that because I have ministered to thousands around the world in my ministry and have seen it time and time again.

How does one get set free from the spirits of Jezebel and Leviathan? It is very hard because those spirits have been entrenched in that person's life for so long that they are very familiar and comfortable with them. They have mindsets that have become a part of them. They act like they are their friends since the person has heard them for a lifetime, but are definitely not in their life to do anything but hurt them and take them to hell. They cause confusion, arguments and strife in marriage and destroy what the Lord put together. Many of those who operate in the church in leadership positions are afflicted with these strong spirits because Jezebel wants them to control other people and stop all effective deliverance from enemy spirits. They are not righteous, nor pure in the Holy Spirit. They are a counterfeit Holy Spirit. The Lord had me release a book in March of 2016 called *Restored to Freedom*, which has been seeing thousands around the world get set free from those spirits.

Unfortunately, more than 75% of marriages around the world are being afflicted by the spirits of Jezebel and Leviathan to some degree, causing strife in marriages and divorce as well as church splits and seeing churches stagnate, shrink and even close. Most authorities state that the divorce rate is higher than 50% in the world but those who are stuck in marriages of misery that have not divorced yet are at least another 25% thus equating to the 75% rate of marriages afflicted by the spirits of Jezebel and Leviathan to some degree. More women than men are tormented by the Jezebel and Leviathan spirits by about a two to one ratio, because girl's hearts get hurt more easily by father wounds than boys. Girls were meant to be loved, cherished and treasured while boys were designed to take more harshness and fight to protect others.

Men also get the Jezebel and Leviathan spirits and are very toxic to the women who struggle to endure the constant verbal barrage and sometimes physical assaults. Many of the women married to men who operate in Jezebel suffer from physical sickness and disease and can die early deaths. The reason behind it all is because the people attracted to those who operate in the Jezebel spirit have the Ahab spirit. They cannot help themselves, just like when the Pied-Piper played his flute and the mind-controlled rodents came a chasing. When you have the Ahab spirit you will automatically be drawn to a strong, controlling person. If you have the Jezebel spirit you will draw to people who you can control. Then once your victim has endured enough of your controlling ways they will separate from you after dealing with the constant strife or arguments.

People who have the Ahab spirit do not like to confront someone who is strong, demanding, bold and may yell at them. They just let things go, trying to keep the peace and put up with a lot of raised voices, ungodly control and abuse. Ahab also likes that the Jezebel spirited people make the hard decisions so they don't have to. They are weak spiritually when it comes to leading. They would rather someone else take charge so if things do not turn out well they will not be the fall guy (or girl). The spirit of Ahab is drawn to someone with the Jezebel spirit, and vice versa. Jezebel wants to control and will be drawn to someone with the Ahab spirit that they can control.

Thus it is very important to recognize early on if your potential spouse grew up with any kind of strong father or mother wounds. That would be the first question I would ask a potential mate because if they did have strong pain from a parent's wounding then they are a probable carrier of the Jezebel and Leviathan spirits. If they had very loving and godly parents then they would not have a spirit of Jezebel / Leviathan or Ahab and usually not desire to marry anyone who had those spirits.

Unfortunately, most people do not connect the dots between parental wounds and how it affects people later in life through developing the spirits of Jezebel and Leviathan. They often times will feel compassion for a person who was hurt without realizing what it does to the person spiritually, emotionally and psychologically. It can devastate a person for life and if you choose to marry someone who has had these strong wounds for a lifetime, then you could be setting yourself up for disaster if you are not careful. So many gentle people who have the spirit of Ahab are drawn towards stronger Alpha type people with the spirit of Jezebel and are abused and don't understand why. They just want to help people and love on them. That is why you see the good girls being drawn to the bad boys. Also this is why you see a lot of the good men being drawn to the controlling and mean women. The spirits of Jezebel and Ahab in them are drawing to each other. Also I have noticed that more physically attractive people struggle with the Jezebel and Ahab spirits. If you have the Jezebel spirit and are attractive, you are able to get more people to do what you want from the opposite sex.

The person who has endured these father and mother wounds are often like a Dr. Jekyll / Mr. Hyde type because they will usually be the life of the party in front of everyone, while being Attila the Hun or Jack the Ripper behind closed doors. You must be aware of this because too many people do not even think about how a person's past dictates how their futures will be. Most everyone in the world who has endured a divorce is because either they or the person they were married to had a father who did not love them unconditionally or worse. It is simply a proven fact.

Therefore, if you know about this up front you will be more cognizant of it in the future when you begin talking to various men and women about potential marriage. Your eyes and ears will be more discerning. You must have this revelation in order to pick a person who is healthy for you or else you will have a marriage filled with misery. There is a statement in the financial world that investment companies must disclose that goes like this "Past results are not indicative of future results." In the case of people I would state that "Past pains are indicative of future hurts." In other words, if you have been hurt deeply by father or mother wounds, then you will normally cause pain for other people and not have unconditional love in your marriage. There is a saying that "Hurting people hurt other people" and that is absolutely true. When a pit bull is being raised in love they will grow up and become playful, loving and fun. But if a pit bull is abused when growing up, they will become fighters and even kill human beings. It is time to be aware of how the enemy operates and to go into your marriage with eyes wide open.

Chapter 3

Breaking Free From Our Pasts

If you or someone you potentially love has endured father or mother wounds, what can be done to make sure you are free from the pain of the past and any spirits associated that have a right to you, so that you can be healthy and choose a healthy mate? The reason this is so important is because if a calm and loving person is operating out of the spirit of Ahab they will be drawn to marry a person who operates from a controlling, manipulative, deceitful and mean spirit of Jezebel. The spirit of Ahab causes a person to not want to confront another person who is louder, more intimidating, demanding and demonstrative. They would rather keep the peace instead of standing up for what they know needs to be done as they will have to engage someone in a verbal battle that they would otherwise choose to let win in order to keep the peace. Wherever you have someone who operates in the Jezebel spirit you will have a spouse who has the Ahab spirit. Thus it is very important that we become set free from both spirits of Jezebel or Ahab (as well as Leviathan) prior to getting married or remarried. Why? Because if you have the Ahab spirit you will unknowingly be drawn to someone with the Jezebel spirit, and vice versa. You will never have peace in your marriage and will wish you never married each other. Have you seen the movie called *The War of the Roses* with Michael Douglas and Kathleen Turner? You do not want that marriage for yourself. You could be married to someone with the subtle version of Jezebel because they were harmed slightly by wounds from childhood, or they could have the extreme version of the spirit of Jezebel due to deep and strong father or mother wounds.

How does one become healed from emotional wounds? Part of it is definitely forgiveness because if you do not forgive those who hurt you then the Lord cannot forgive you for your sins. Mark 11:25-26 NKJV states "[25] And whenever you stand praying, if you have anything against anyone, forgive him, that your Father in heaven may also forgive you your trespasses. [26] But if you do not forgive, neither will your Father in heaven forgive your trespasses."

In this chapter we will focus on getting people freed from generational curses, spirits of Jezebel, Leviathan and Ahab. I have listed some very powerful and proven effective prayers in my book *Restored to Freedom* which have been setting people free from the spirits of Jezebel / Leviathan at astounding numbers around the world. I also have a book called *Waking The Lion Within,* which has helped people get delivered from the spirit of Ahab. When people pray the renunciation prayers in the books most feel the spirits lift and they become the people whom the Lord created them to be. They are now able to become a mighty man or woman of valor. They also become more pure, righteous and godly in the Lord. They actually feel lighter as the heaviness of those dark spirits leave. Many get healed from various pains, sicknesses and diseases.

If you feel that you have strong spirits of Jezebel / Leviathan or Ahab then I would strongly suggest you read both of my books in order to understand and have revelation in your spirit. You need to have the full revelation of those spirits in order to be set free from them. Then you need to read the renunciation prayers to get completely delivered. If you still are affected by spirits of fear, anxiety or depression you may need to read the *Restored to Freedom* book again as well as the renunciation prayers of deliverance.

On the next few pages I am listing all the renunciation prayers in order for you to take your authority and gain freedom from the spirits. Make sure that you are in a quiet place and be in a mindset of reverence and fervency. When you truly mean these prayers with all your heart you will see miraculous changes in your life and future marriage. If you are not solemn and do not mean it with all of your heart then you may have to read them again later, and even again. The enemy knows if you mean it or not and will not want to give up ground easily. Many when reading the following prayers will sense the spirits being broken off as some will "yawn", "burp" or feel a tingling sensation or even that the spirits are trying to cause them not to read the prayers (pressure on their chests or necks).

Prayer to Break Off Generational Curses

I break all curses or vows that have ever been spoken over me from my mother and father and from all generational curses that have been spoken over anyone in my ancestry all the way back to Adam and Eve.

In Jesus Christ's name I declare that I am not in agreement with any form of sin, or disobedience that operates in this world and against the throne of God, as I am not in agreement to any person, or family member who deliberately sinned, or perverted God's ways. In the Mighty name of Jesus Christ I thank You Father God for Your good and righteous ways and I seek to live my life by Your Spirit and reap the rewards of living by Your righteousness.

I repent for every relative connected to my family ancestry who has deliberately, or without spiritual wisdom sinned against my Lord, or His people. I realize that all sin will be judged one day and that each one of us is accountable for what we have said, or done, but I am repenting for my families sins in that I shall be released from any curses these sins may have produced against me. I put all of my sins and my ancestors' sins at the foot of the cross and declare that Jesus Christ has paid the price and that Father God you have forgiven us for all.

I break all generational curses of pride, lust, perversion, rebellion, witchcraft, occult activity, idolatry, poverty, sickness, infirmity, disease, rejection, fear, confusion, addiction, death, and destruction in the name and by the blood of Jesus.

I curse all traumas in my ancestors and descendants lives that have had any right to me and command all memory of these to be forever forgotten and never remembered again. I replace these traumas with peace. I speak that any and all nightmares in sleep will be turned to joy and loving dreams and visions from the Lord.

I renounce the behavior of any relative in our family background who has lived more for the world, than for God. I renounce any ungodly beliefs, traditions, rituals, or customs that my people may have followed or acted upon. I repent of those family members who sought to fulfill the selfishness of their desires, and those who have perverted God's righteousness for I myself choose to serve God and live by His ways.

I declare that my descendants will receive blessings and favor from this day forward. That we will be blessed with love, joy and peace throughout our lives and that Jesus will be the King of our lives. I declare life and health to me and all in my family line in Jesus mighty name!

Amen.

Prayer to Renounce the Jezebel Spirit

Heavenly Father,

I come before you with a contrite, humble, and sincere heart. Thank you for having my eyes opened and scales removed today to the truth of what I have been battling in my life. I was truly a victim of my circumstances as I was an innocent child that was being controlled, manipulated and hurt through my father (and/or mother) as they were hurt by the enemy through their parents as did their ancestors as the pain and abuse was a vicious cycle that will now be broken over my life and all of my descendants. I am ready for this controlling spirit to be broken off of my life once and for all. Today I take back what the enemy has stolen from me and I command all painful memories of my past to be removed forever, never to be remembered again. I forgive all that have hurt me in my past and break off all spirits of offense that I have taken. I choose to forgive my father for all that he did to hurt me. I choose to forgive my mother for all that she did to hurt me (and you should name anyone else that has hurt you as there is power and healing in forgiveness).

I cancel every negative, unscriptural word ever spoken over my life and all physical, emotional or sexual acts that have hurt me throughout my lifetime. I break the power of the spirits of confusion, fear, control, anger, deceit, pride, arrogance and manipulation and exchange all hurts and pains from my past to be taken by Jesus Christ and forever healed and replaced with His love, joy and peace for the remainder of my days on earth. I command all the effects from serving the spirit of Jezebel to be broken off of me and my descendants forever.

I command every demonic influence of any name from the spirit of Jezebel to be broken off of my life and I truly repent for my serving of these spirits intentionally or inadvertently. I renounce all wrong associations that I've had which served the spirit of Jezebel. I repent for all those that I have hurt with my controlling behavior and declare that I will no longer serve the powers of witchcraft from this moment forward. I declare a divorce with the spirit of Jezebel. I want nothing to do with the wickedness of that spirit in my life and declare that I will serve only the one true and living God with all of my being.

All the wounds that Jesus took for me on the cross were sufficient for me to be healed forever and I exchange my broken heart for a new heart that is soft, gentle, loving, pure, and strong (symbolically pull a knife out of your old heart and replace your heart with a new one from your heavenly Papa who loves you unconditionally).

I declare that I will serve Jesus Christ and His Word with all of my heart from this moment forward. I declare I will not compromise my living to any standard below Christ's love, purity, and Holiness. Thank you, Jesus, for healing my broken heart forevermore and giving me a new life to serve you with.
In Jesus blessed name. Amen!

Next just rest and take several deep breaths with your new clean and pure heart and receive the peace from your loving Papa Father. You should feel the weight of the world lifted from your shoulders and feel a tremendous peace like you may have never felt before. There is power in your words and life and death is in the power of your tongue.

<u>Prayer to Renounce the Spirit of Ahab</u>

Father in Heaven, I come to You in the name of Jesus Christ, my Savior and Lord. Father, it is my desire to see Your Kingdom come into my life and into my marriage (or future marriage) and my family in a new and powerful way. Right now I make a decision to forgive any and everyone who has had influence in my life to cause me to be less than the person of God You wanted me to be. Father, I forgive the following persons who have unfairly controlled me (name anyone who comes to mind).

I repent of operating in the Ahab spirit and ask You to forgive me. I now take back the authority and responsibility You have given to me that I relinquished to Jezebel. By the power that works in me according to Your strength and anointing, I will watch over and minister to my new husband or wife in Christ and my children. Father, I ask for wisdom and guidance as I do this.

In the name of Jesus Christ, I break every curse that has come upon me or been spoken over me and my family because of the influence of the Spirit of Jezebel within my husband or wife and any sins of ours or our ancestors. I command every evil spirit that has come in through curses that I or others have spoken over me to leave me. Go out of me, now, in the name of Jesus Christ! You must also loose my (husband or wife) and family. I say to you evil spirits, Go! I declare that I am bold in the Lord and command restoration of everything that the Spirit of Jezebel has done to hurt me. I am blessed and highly favored and am strong in the Lord and decree that my future life will be far greater than my former. As a believer in Jesus Christ I have been granted the same authority as Christ and declare divine health throughout every cell in my body. I have the mind of Christ! I will help others that I know to become free from every Spirit of Jezebel and Spirit of Ahab and decree that I will have a strong anointing over those spirits the rest of my life.

Thank You Father for deliverance and healing, now and in the days to come. I Praise Your Holy Name. Amen!

Prayer to Renounce the Leviathan Spirit

Lord, I come before you with a humble and contrite spirit and command all spirits of pride to be gone from me forever in Jesus name. I ask you God to remove from my life any influence from the spirit of Leviathan. I reject this spirit completely with all my heart and command it to be broken off me forever, never to return. Forgive me for any ways that I have served this spirit either intentionally or inadvertently. Forgive me for any ways in which I have been twisted or have twisted the truth, that I have listened to distortion of the truth or have distorted the truth. I devote myself to bringing unity, not division or confusion, into the church and in my personal relationships and will therefore honor other Godly members and those you have placed in authority over me.

It states in Isaiah 27:1 *"In that day the Lord with His severe sword, great and strong, will punish Leviathan the fleeing serpent, Leviathan that twisted serpent; And He will slay the reptile that is in the sea".* I declare that Leviathan is severed from my life now and forever more. By your grace I will speak the truth in love and dedicate myself to expressing the truth of your word in my life, and have a humble and contrite spirit in the precious name of Jesus. Amen."

I command Leviathan's head, body and tail be completely gone from my body and send you to hell in Jesus name! I declare that my back, discs and spine be completely aligned perfectly and any organs are untwisted and made perfect. I also speak to my legs that they are both the exact same length in Jesus name. I declare that I will sleep soundly at night and have prophetic dreams. When I read the Word or listen to it I will not fall asleep but retain everything that I read or hear. All sickness and disease in my body be gone now and I declare every cell in my body be completely healed. Thank you Jesus!

Chapter 4

What To Do When You Are Waiting

So once you have been delivered from all generational curses and spirits of Jezebel, Leviathan and Ahab and healed from any entrenched mindsets from your past wounds, what should you do when waiting to find your husband or wife? There are many who choose to get on dating sites and pursue people from the opposite sex and have conversations frequently with people who are not healthy. The challenge is that you will soon wear yourself out after talking to each person and trying to juggle multiple conversations via Facebook Messenger / Instagram / Texts / FaceTime.

I know of some women who have thousands of wolves that are trying to pursue them. The men act all 'godly' if they know that they profess to be a Christian, but in reality they are nothing more than wolves in sheep's clothing. They try to tell them what they want to hear so they will fall in love with them. So what most do is pick a few men who look attractive to them and then begin conversations with them. The challenge is with some who live farther away such as several states away or in another country. Without spending regular physical time with them you will not know who they really are. Even then it could take months of going down the road with a man or woman who later finally proves to have worn a mask the entire time as they are not who they represented themselves to be at the start of the relationship, thus wasting your time, money and breaking your heart.

Therefore I recommend doing the following while waiting to find Mr. or Mrs. Right:

- Spending time in prayer / praying in tongues of around an hour throughout the day. Your spirit will become stronger against your flesh and you will draw closer to the Lord. When you spend more time with the Lord you will feel the peace that passes all understanding and not be driven out of fear and your flesh to compromise your values or operate out of your fleshly desires. You also will increase your level of discernment spiritually when you meet a potential future spouse candidate and have a higher level of discernment if they are a godly mate or a fake.

- Read your Bible which will allow you to learn more how to live and become more like Christ. When you fill your mind with scripture you will become godly and become stronger in the spirit.

- Go on an extended fast from food and any other things that the Lord leads – this causes your spirit man (or woman) to get stronger against your flesh and draws you into more peace with the Lord so you can hear even more clearly. You do not want to have any fleshly desires that could cause the enemy in a fake mate to pull you in to them.

- Remain sexually pure at all times. This includes not looking at women or men lustfully nor masturbating. When you act out sexually you stop the ability of the Lord to bless you. You also open up the door to the enemy to have a legal right to hurt you. When you sin sexually you walk farther away from the Lord and not closer.

- Play praise / worship / soaking music when you drive. When your mind is staid on things of the Lord the enemy will not be able to speak to you as easily. Instead of crying out to desire a man or woman to complete you, you will be in a state of more peace.

- Go for walks or do activities in and around nature. Take hikes, kayaks or canoe trips on lakes or rivers, walks on trails, etc. When you are around nature you will feel the peace of the Lord more around you. You will also be able to hear the Lord more clearly for direction and feel His presence.

- Ask the Lord for direction instead of talking to a number of people and getting their human opinions. The Lord knows what you need. Often times your future spouse needs to be healed from their wounds and is not ready yet for you to be introduced to. Therefore work on getting yourself healed and ready for your future husband or wife. Also if you do talk to anyone you need to be honest with them. Some people who have the spirit of Jezebel very strongly will never admit that they did some very evil things and blame their spouse for everything.

- Focus on a hobby that you enjoy as it will allow you to take time for things that are healthy. I always recommend people to exercise because that will keep your temple in good shape, help you look more healthy, give you more energy and you will sleep much better at night.

- Eat healthy. If you eat a lot of sugar, fried or fatty foods, then you will feel sluggish, more depressed and negative. Everything in balance is good but the more fresh foods, fruits and vegetables and water you put in your body, the better you will feel.

- Read godly books that will help you grow spiritually instead of watching secular TV and wasting your time on things that will pull you away from growing in the spirit. So many people waste hours a day watching TV programs that will never improve their lives. Then when they are 50, 60 or 70 years of age, their best years of life are gone. No one ever said on their death bed "I wish I could have watched more Family Feud, Jeopardy or Jerry Springer show episodes."

- Attend a good spirit-led church or ministry in order to be around healthy, godly people that will encourage you positively. If you have friends around you who are not godly, they will influence you negatively and cause you to get off the right track. So make sure to surround yourself with an inner circle of godly friends who hear from the Lord.

- Do something that you have never been able to do before but have always wanted. Crochet or knit a blanket, paint a beautiful picture, visit a place you have always wanted to, take a ride in a powered parachute, hot air balloon, run a 5k race or marathon, etc.

- Write a book that you have always wanted to but never had the time before. Anyone can write books today using self-publishers like CreateSpace by Amazon and others. The Lord wants you to be creative and share your testimonies and things that you have experienced in life so others can learn from you.

- Focus more on helping others and you will ultimately learn to become more like Christ. There are so many people around the world who are hurting due to some strong pains from their fathers or mothers, and when you take the focus off of yourself and instead focus on others you will develop a better picture of how the Lord wants to use you in ministry.

- Explore a place that you never have visited before. There is something about taking a new adventure in life that is exciting to do. God wants us to take adventures in life and to visit places we have never gone before. You will feel alive when you experience something that you have never seen or experienced before.

- Get involved with a small group at your church and do street ministry, prophesy over random people, heal the sick, help people become freed from demonic spirits. There is nothing like doing what Jesus wants us to do.

- Listen to praise and worship music throughout your apartment or home as either background music or turn it up and get your praise and worship on. There is nothing that can change the atmosphere in your home like cranking the music up.

- Spend more time talking to same sex friends than opposite sex friends. If you talk more to the opposite sex then you will be more tempted to draw to them in an unhealthy relationship instead of getting completely healed from your past hurts and broken relationships

- Ask the Lord if He wants you to start a ministry. Often times the Lord will bring you into a ministry during your time of singleness because you can focus all of your time and energy on it as your attention is not divided. Then once you have started the ministry He will bring you a helpmate to come along side of you and then later can lead to a beautiful ministry together as your hearts will be as one.

- The greatest times of growth often come through adversity in life. Spend much of your time by yourself with the Lord and see where He leads you. The Lord wants you all to Himself and since you have the time now to take advantage of it, you need to.

- Visit with people that you have not seen for a long time. Old friends, family members, people that you have missed.

- Take a new school of ministry class in the prophetic, healing or deliverance area. Grow yourself spiritually.

- Write a song and either record yourself singing it or have someone else sing it. The Lord loves to develop your musical and artistic talents.

- Spend a couple of days in a cabin in the woods getting away privately with the Lord. Let the Lord speak to you and through you and record what you hear Him say to you.

Chapter 5

Warning Signs of Mr. and Mrs. Wrong

Many people want to fast forward the process of finding their future spouse instead of waiting on the Lord's timing (which, by the way, is always longer than our timing, if you haven't noticed). Of course part of the Lord's timing is dealing with our own stuff and getting healed and delivered before getting connected to someone who has their own stuff. Some younger Christians have chosen to go to secular places such as dance clubs or bars, but if you choose to lower your Christian standards you will not find a truly godly woman or man and be in worse shape than when you began. Some have attended larger, non-denominational, watered-down message churches because they tend to have more people who attend, thus they have more single people to choose from (does not take a B.S. in Engineering to compute the logic of that). Unfortunately, you may also water down your chances of finding a person who is truly spiritually strong in the Lord because many who attend the larger churches do not operate in the stronger giftings of the Lord. They can blend in better and hide the darker side of themselves because others that attend many larger churches are not as discerning in the spirit. The larger churches will usually not talk about things like getting people delivered from demonic spirits, thus they will never get people set free from the Jezebel / Leviathan or Ahab spirits. They may talk about praying in tongues but usually do not operate in it regularly or openly. They usually will not prophesy over people as well. Not every larger church is the same so just be aware.

Of course, if you are not personally strong in the Lord and do not want a man or woman who is very strong in the Lord, then that might be the perfect place for you. It just depends on how godly of a man or woman that you really want and how long you are willing to wait for the process to play out. The goal of this book is to help you find a strong, godly mate and not a person who says and does godly things before marriage but then once they have you, transform back into a controlling, manipulative and enemy-controlled liar. Who wants to be married to a Pharisee?

If you want a truly godly man or woman, then you may not find who you are looking for in the same places that the masses of people are congregating. You will definitely find a lot of people to choose from in a larger venue, but usually the messages that are preached will be such that they appeal to the broader audiences so could not have as much meat and depth. I am not saying all large churches speak watered down messages, but many do. A man or woman who is pursuing the Lord in a much deeper way will often attend churches or ministries that are focused on the deeper teachings and flow in more of the gifting's openly. They may be a part of a small but growing church or ministry or even have their own ministry. They will spend time reading the Word for themselves and have it deep in their hearts. They will pray in tongues often, may fast food on occasion, and hear the Lord clearly and do what the Lord directs. They will not be proud or arrogant and brag on themselves as those are clearly not fruits of the spirit but of the enemy. They will usually have others promoting or praising them and the spirit of the Lord will highlight them to you. Sometimes you will not even have to look for them as the Lord will connect you divinely and then confirm it with other godly men or women or He may give you prophetic dreams. He wants to give you the desires of your heart if only you are patient.

When the Lord wants you to connect with your future mate, He will do it in such a way that you will have no doubts as you will feel His peace. The more that you try to make it happen yourself, the more the enemy will be able to send you a counterfeit Boaz or Esther. I have talked to so many people around the world who have told me that there were warning signs but something in them could not stop the process for going forward. One man from California told me that he wanted to break off his engagement to his potential wife but she talked to his godly parents and got them to coerce him to reconsider and marry her. Just months after he said 'I do" he knew he made a horrible mistake. Then after they had a child she became even worse. His heart is breaking because he knew he should not have married her in the first place, but now he is living a life that he never has peace and is constantly tormented. Unfortunately, he had the Ahab spirit and could not stand up to her and say "No!" and walk away from her. Now he has to decide if she refuses to admit that she has the Jezebel spirit if he will stay married to her or not.

I have seen some people who stated that they were led to attend a certain singles group event or a place where they knew single people were going to be meeting at looking for love. Then they would start to manufacture excuses and ignore warning signs to start dating a person they had no business dating. Facebook is becoming more of a dangerous place to connect with people easily from the opposite sex because people will see your picture and request to be friends and then start to say nice things to you and you have no idea if they are a lying, narcissistic, Jezebel or not.

One man said that his former Jezebel girlfriend spoke to him shortly after connecting with him and said "The Lord told me that you were my future husband." Unfortunately she used that as a way to manipulate the man who was in ministry into trying to get him to marry her as he was a challenge for her to conquer as she saw him as a potential successful husband in ministry to make her look good. At the time he had the Ahab spirit and fell for her, but later he saw her do some sexually perverse, controlling, manipulative and even scary things as her Jezebel spirit began to be exposed as time went on because she could no longer keep it hidden. Time has a way of exposing the truth that is buried deep inside of a person. Always ask the Lord for a personal confirmation or revelation and He will give it to you. Also be cautious with people who give you a personal prophetic word in which it can be interpreted that they are your future mate or ministry partner as they could be trying to manipulate you to do what they want.

In the past, dating websites were the main venue to find people who were on the market and interested in dating someone. Today social media has largely taken that place. Facebook is so easy to find someone who is attractive. Assuming their profile picture has not been filtered and modified to misrepresent a person's actual looks – people can find you very easily and quickly. To begin a conversation with a total stranger now is as easy as sending them a private message using Facebook Messenger. No longer do you have to email or plead with them for a cell phone number so you can text and call them. You can simply send a message to anyone in the world now by going to Facebook. There was a funny quote I saw the other day that stated this: "Facebook. Helping Stalkers Since 2004." This is so true as people can follow your personal life as soon as you allow them to become your friend (and even before then if your profile is listed as public on Facebook).

78

Some people who operate from a Jezebel spirit will actually observe another person's likes and dislikes on Facebook, so then over time they will know what they like or do not like before they move in to try to reel them in. Then over time when they initiate discussions with their victim they become what their victim wanted them to be. Then after moving in to engage their victim in conversation, they appear to be their soulmate. Then they became who their victim wanted them to be and their victim begins to fall in love with themself, unconsciously. They cannot believe all the things that they have in common. One man noticed a certain picture that a woman had in her apartment in a photo on Facebook and then when he was at someone else's place he commented how they had the exact same picture and how it must be some kind of destiny thing for them as it was a sign from the Lord (not). He was a master at trying to manufacture things into some kind of spiritual confirmation to manipulate that God was in this potential relationship.

Be very careful of people who draw you in quickly and tell you that they love you soon after they just meet you. This is called "love bombing" as they throw that word out there soon in order to draw you in. Many time the higher level Jezebel men will do this to women because they know that they can play on their emotions. Then before long the women will want to marry them because they feel like this is their knight in shining armor and the women feel that the men are their destinies. Sometimes they will tell you that "The Lord told me that we will be married and do ministry together." Be very careful of long distance relationships because people are able to conceal any darkness about themselves more easily because you will not see them as often.

Those who operate in the higher level spectrum of the Jezebel spirit would be labeled in the psychological community as a narcissist. Those with a narcissistic personality are characterized by their persistent grandiosity, excessive need for admiration, and a disdain and lack of empathy for others. These individuals often display arrogance, a sense of superiority, and power-seeking behaviors. They disregard the feelings of others and expect to be treated as superior regardless of their actual status or achievements. They usually have fragile egos, an inability to tolerate criticism, and a tendency to belittle others in an attempt to validate their own superiority. Spiritually, the narcissist person operates in the spirit of Jezebel at a very strong level. If you do not do what he or she demands then they will get angry with you and can often lead them to violence and your very life could be in danger.

One young woman who has a strong prophetic call on her life recently was drawn to a man who slowly began to control and manipulate her over time. He pulled her into a business venture with him and little by little had her paying for a new $750 iPhone for him, a new joint cell phone plan, other monthly bills and before she knew it in just a couple of months she had over $20,000 in total debt because of him. He started telling her that her calling from the Lord of going into full time ministry was not going to happen and she just needed to go back to school and get a regular business job. He even mentioned to her that it only costs $400 to kill someone and had inferred if she ever left him for another boyfriend that he may have to do something about it. Finally she broke things off with him but has to be concerned if this man will do something to try to hurt her or say lies about her.

One man married a woman with two sons and he paid for over $85,000 worth of bills and expenses that her sons could not afford. He went into debt of $50,000 for her sons. Then she divorced him after he finally had to separate from her due to her controlling and abusive ways. Finally, she kept his $12,000 diamond that he earned from his company years before they married and also took all of the thousands of dollars he spent to fix up her house and furnishings as well as other property that he owned before marriage. She had no conscious whatsoever, and lied about him to try to make her look good and him bad.

One man had married but had lost his wife to death. He then remarried a girl who used to be a cheerleader in high school and he always thought was pretty. Unfortunately after marriage she turned on him and his daughter and created such a toxic environment that he had to separate. She then began whispering lies about him and his daughter to their church and immediately there was dissension between the members. One of the elders of the church believed the lies of the man's wife and said he "got a word" from the Lord and told him he needed to go back to his wife and put her first ahead of his daughter. Unfortunately this was very bad advice as the daughter had been hurt greatly through the words of her Jezebel stepmother. People need to wake up and discern the truth as so many who have the Jezebel spirit are so good at lying that they can turn an entire church against a godly man or vice versa.

One man who had loved his extreme Jezebel wife for six years finally was released to leave her after much verbal, physical and sexual abuse. His wife lied to the senior pastor and other leaders in the church about him and the senior pastor kicked him out of the church. Then the pastor actually encouraged the man's wife to divorce him (which was her 4th divorce in her life with the previous marriages lasting 5 years, 2 years and 14 months) instead of getting her delivered and holding her accountable. The man had a dream when his wife's divorce was officially signed and in the dream he saw her pastor's church with only 25 people attending it. They had about 200 at the time of the dream. The Lord told him when he woke up that her church would be shut down because the senior pastor and much of his leaders and those attending operated in the Jezebel spirit. The man eventually told the pastor that he needed to repent for speaking to his congregation that there was no such thing as a Jezebel spirit and also said that if people died and went to hell that God would give them one more chance to get out of hell and called it the 2nd Judgment in Revelation.

The pastor mocked the man and continued his arrogant ways. A year later his church dropped to 25 people and was soon after sold to the humane society. The Lord told the man that just like Jezebel was eaten by the dogs - that the church was also sold to the dogs.

The pastor was no longer a pastor after that. The Lord said that He was going to shut down more churches where the senior pastor either had the Jezebel spirit or was tolerating others in his church leadership who operated in the Jezebel spirit.

The Welsh revival in 1904 saw over 100,000 souls come to the Lord through a young man named Evan Roberts but he was conquered by a Jezebel controlled woman named Jesse Penn-Lewis who seduced and deceived the revivalist in the prime of his anointing in the early 1920's. She sought to ride on Roberts' coattails and flattered him with her words that tried to ease the pain he was suffering from the religious spirits coming against the revival. But her smooth words hurt and did not help him. He suffered a nervous breakdown and was confined to a bed for more than a year and he allowed his wife to decide who he would see and what he would do. She wrote a book called "War on the Saints" that he later denounced. Her doctrine was largely rejected in Wales. Although Roberts lived to 72 he ceased preaching in his early 20's. Jezebel hates the move of the Holy Spirit and shut the revival down just as it was really starting to move powerfully.

These are very common scenarios of what is happening between men and women around the world every day today. The Jezebel spirit will pull in the person with the Ahab spirit and take them for all they can get away with and they will not feel any conviction for the evil that they are doing. There are so many broken hearted Ahab victims around the world who don't know what happened to them in their marriages and lives. It is time for people to wake up to what is really going on out there in the dating and marriage world. If you choose to marry someone with the Jezebel spirit, you will be hurt and never have peace. Most who operate in the spirit of Jezebel are very sly, often physically attractive and know how to reel in their victims. It does not matter how physically attractive a woman or man is if they have a heart that is filled full of control, manipulation, anger, hatred and vitriol. Just look at all the beautiful people in Hollywood. They are largely miserable and get divorced frequently or live in pure misery of constant strive.

I received a call from a doctor who lived in Kentucky during the summer of 2017. He told me that he had listened to a Podcast interview I had done with Charisma magazine. He said it explained his situation perfectly with his wife. She was beautiful and he loved her with all his heart, but she was horribly controlling to him and made his life miserable every day. He did not know what to do to fix her so was going to try to get her a copy of my book *Restored to Freedom* by sending it from Amazon as a gift so she would not know who sent it to her. After I talked to him the Lord spoke to me and asked me how many physicians operated out of an Ahab spirit who were married to people with the Jezebel spirit. I had never thought about it before. I responded to the Lord with "Probably a lot" and He said "Exactly." So if you know of any doctors or potential doctors, you may want to give them a copy of this book or my *Restored to Freedom* book to help them know what they are dealing with.

There are many of these types of men and women all over the world. Those who operate out of the Jezebel spirit are often times charismatic, outgoing, life of the parties and everyone would say how lucky you were to have found them. But deep inside they have a very dark and sinister side that turns out to not be a good mate at all and an even worse friend. They are out for themselves only and want to use you to help them accomplish their selfish goals. They look for people to take advantage of who are innocent, loving and physically attractive in order to make themselves look good and gain more power or control. If a physically attractive man has the Jezebel spirit he will usually look at finding a physically attractive woman that can make him look good to others. Sort of like a "trophy" wife that others will think how successful he is in life. And a woman who has Jezebel will often look for a wealthy, successful man who behaves calmly and is easy to control.

That is why it is so critical for people to be freed completely from the Ahab spirit before they attempt to look for a potential mate, because if they don't then they will be drawn to a person with the spirit of Jezebel and set themselves up for either a lifetime of pain and control or a divorce. Freedom from the Ahab spirit will allow you to see in the spirit who people really are inside their spirits and not be duped into just looking at the outer mask of beauty they are wearing. I have talked to thousands of people around the world who have endured marriages to those with the Jezebel spirit and they have all confirmed if they had it to do again, knowing now about the spirit of Jezebel that they would never again choose based on physical looks but by discerning who the person really is inside their heart. An example of how God selects a man or woman not being based on their outward appearance, but the heart is in 1 Samuel 16:7 NKJV "But the Lord said to Samuel, "Do not look at his appearance or at his physical stature, because I have refused him. For the Lord does not see as man sees; for man looks at the outward appearance, but the Lord looks at the heart."

So what I am trying to convey is that many decide on who they are going to marry based largely on their outward appearance physically and ignore all the red flags that they pick up on with their hearts / spirits during the dating process. If all you want is someone who is a plain vanilla Christian, who has various sin in their lives, then you can settle for anyone. If you truly want a man or woman on fire for God who is pure and righteous, then you will need to have the Lord direct you to them. He will do it and will also confirm it through either other people who don't know you or through dreams or other personal ways. When you try to make it happen by attending groups looking specifically for single women or men, then often times you could get someone who has not been set free from past enemy spirits yet and needs to go through deliverance.

It is extremely important to not ignore the "red flags" that the Holy Spirit will show you along the dating journey. If you have historically operated out of the spirit of Ahab where you are usually calm and do not like confrontation then you will be drawn to a higher energy person who is the life of the party and can have the more controlling Jezebel spirit. Below are some signs to look for if a person may have the spirit of Jezebel:

- They appear to be very confident yet are usually anxious underneath and do not walk in peace very often.

- Their appearance to look confident to the public is actually over-confidence to cover up for their insecurity deep inside.

- They usually will have a high energy level most of the time which will draw you and others to them. They are often the "life of the party" types.

- They will usually act like they are very godly and spiritual, indicating that they read their bible a lot, fast and pray, worship, even pray in tongues while most of it is a lie. You need to see consistent actions that naturally flow from them and not occasional acts yet making excuses constantly.

- They will state or do various things with you early on in the relationship that they know you want to hear or do because they could have studied your likes and dislikes on Facebook or other social media. Given enough time you will see that they will not want to do things with you once they believe they have you as a potential spouse.

- They usually cannot look you in the eye very long because the enemy spirit within them causes them to sense that you could be on to their lying ways and will look away frequently. They have limited to no conscience for deceiving and lying.

- They may tell you that they "love you" within a few dates or times talking on the phone and flatter you. This is referred to as "love bombing" as they will throw it out to you early and often to pull you in to them.

- They will usually have a dark sexual side of them that will either crave sex or control you later with limiting you on sex. They are master manipulators in this department. They may tell you things to turn you on sexually such as "When I drink alcohol all my clothes come off," or "I enjoy oral sex, how about you?", or they will touch your body in ways to turn you on and want to French kiss you early on.

- They are masters at lying so you need to date them over a longer period of time before marrying because they cannot keep the mask on all the time and will eventually show their true colors. They may indicate that they are financially well off when they are a mess. They may suck you in by getting you to feel sorry for them and pay for things that they cannot afford.

- They are very selfish and self-absorbed only thinking of things that can benefit them. They do not care about what your needs and desires are. They may want to watch a movie that is not godly and care less if it causes you to be hurt or in fear.

- After a longer period of time if you do not give them their way, then they will become angry and often change the tone of their voice to a more sinister and controlling, manipulative way. They could become angry with you eventually and say things like "If you ever do that again I will hurt you!"

- Over time you will see that they are jealous of people from the opposite sex having conversations with you because they want to own you all to themselves. One man's wife forbid him to give prophetic words from the Lord to women who came up to worship with men at the beginning of worship.

- They are usually prideful and arrogant and will expect you to do whatever they want. You will feel like they think they are the most attractive person on earth and you should feel honored that they are spending time with you and desire you.

- They treat people who cannot do anything for them very poorly with disregard and do not want to waste their time with anyone who cannot benefit them.

- They will usually have had a poor relationship with their father or mother and usually would have been unloved, rejected or controlled in a way that hurt them deeply.

- They can become angry easily and quickly if they do not get their own way.

- They may attempt to "gaslight" you. This is a form of intimidation or psychological abuse, sometimes called ambient abuse where false information is presented to you, making you doubt your own memory, perception and sanity. They will switch something around on someone that you know, but then deny knowing anything about it, and to explain that you must be imagining things when you challenge them. It is an increasing frequency of systematically withholding factual information from or providing false information to you, causing you to feel anxious, confused and less able to trust your own memory and perception. An example is that they may tell you things that never really happened such as they say, "I told you last week that I was going to meet with my friends to go shopping, but you didn't remember it."

- They will usually have a leadership position because they love to tell other people what to do and control them.

If you have been set free from the Jezebel spirit then you will tend to gravitate towards someone with the spirit of Ahab. The various traits of the Ahab spirit are as follows:

- They are usually very passive when it comes to making decisions, deferring to other people and thinking the best of everyone. Usually very innocent who is a prime target of Jezebel.

- They are not strong spiritual leaders and have a hard time taking the lead with reading the Bible as a couple, praying in tongues as a couple, and leading by example.

- They may have a secret addiction to pornography.

- If they are men they will use women to get what they want.

- Does not want to be bothered to have to take on any new responsibilities in life.

- Tends to be successful in business ventures, making good money and work ethic.

- They have a hard time with confronting people who need to be confronted and allow things to happen to avoid a potential confrontation out of the fear that they will be yelled at or dominated.

- They are more laid back in their personality and easy going, which makes them easier to control.

- Become cry-babies to get people to feel sorry for them and do what they want.

- They often times will be funny and tell jokes as this keeps the situation light and not as serious, thus they don't have to deal with things in their own life or with others that have given them pain deep down inside.

So when you are looking for Mr. and Mrs. Right by looking for them through pure eyes, unblemished from the spirits of Jezebel or Ahab, you will find them more easily without having to search every social media and dating site and church on earth. The Lord will bring them to you as you are now healed and in the right mindset. When you stop doing the searching He will bring them to you in His perfect timing and make sure that they are also healed and delivered from their pasts. Too many people try to make things happen in their own power instead of letting the process of purifying work in their lives. Always keep this in mind....once you are married you can no longer do whatever you want as you will need to ask your spouse and mutually decide. Give it time and relax in the process. Do not rush it or you will make a mistake and marry someone that the enemy wanted for you.

Chapter 6

Marrying Your Best Friend

Once you have found someone who could potentially be Mr. or Mrs. Right, how do you really know who they are before marrying them? One would hope that you actually have a lot in common with them and that your conversations will just flow without any effort for either of you in having to cover up any negative truth of both of your lives. You should be able to be transparent with them about your past and not feel judged. You will not have to change into becoming a person that they want to fall in love with, as you will just be who you are and they will love you because of who you actually are. I always say that if you can talk with them for hours but it only seems like minutes, and you rarely ever get into any disagreements with them after many months of key discussions, then chances are you will be able to enjoy your life together in marriage. You will usually be able to discern in the spirit who they really are as long as you are free from the spirit of Ahab /

Jezebel / and Leviathan. The true test of any relationship is time and enduring several stressful situations in life together.

If you barely spend any time with the person because they live far away, then that person can act nice around you during the brief times of togetherness. But then you never really know how they are on a day to day basis. If you have spent many months around them or years, and you have experienced few arguments and when you do have a disagreement you are able to talk it through calmly, then you will usually have success in marriage. You should feel loved and not lusted after or controlled. But if they have a mean tone, twist the truth, blame you, cause you to feel stupid, send you sexual texts or videos or pictures, then it would be best to cut it off and move on quickly. If they are behaving that way before marriage, it will be a hundred times worse after they have you (own you).

It is always hard for a person who operates in the Ahab spirit to break a relationship off from a person with the Jezebel spirit, often times because they know it will bring up a confrontation of words and the Ahab in you would rather just let it go and get married. Unfortunately you will eventually be dominated with a life of misery and wished you had stood up for yourself. So how can you discern what a healthy picture of a future marriage relationship looks like? I list below some of the more healthy traits of what a true, best friend would look like.

Healthy traits of what a best friend picture looks like:

- You allow the relationship to progress slowly over several months and one person does not pressure or control the other. Then the relationship will grow from acquaintances to friends to best friends.

- You both put Christ first before each other and have a personal relationship with Christ. You spend time alone with the Lord and hear the Lord for yourself and can then come together and share what you each have heard. It is important that you alternate who shares first because if a person has the Jezebel spirit then he or she will echo whatever you state that you heard in order to try to pull you towards them.

- You enjoy reading the Word together and having healthy discussions of how the Word applies to your daily walk. The man will want to lead his wife spiritually and the woman will submit to his leadership.

- You genuinely enjoy praying together and it is not an effort to do it (and pray in tongues together as that draws you more closely in one spirit which is true Agape love intimacy).

- You talk a lot with no arguments and when you do have a disagreement you are both calm and come to a mutually agreeable resolution. If you constantly are getting into contentions or strife then you will not be a good fit in marriage.

- The man opens the car door and other doors for the woman. The man treats the woman like a princess. The woman does not treat the man with any contempt or boss him around telling him what to do.

- You laugh together often. Laughing is a great way to enjoy your friend (as long as you are not laughing at the expense of each other). The Bible talks about how laughter is good medicine for the soul. Medically laughter lowers your blood pressure, reduces stress hormones, improves cardiac health, strengthens your abdominal muscles, triggers the release of endorphins, and boosts T-cells.

- You are both pure sexually with no hidden sin in your life. This is very important because if one or both of you are struggling with being honest and pure sexually prior to marriage then it will only get worse once you are married. You will love each other in a very pure, innocent and godly sense.

- You will have a lot of similar interests in life – you both enjoy doing things together much of the time. Over time you will continue to want to be together and bring life into others' lives. If one person wants to go shooting guns and riding ATVs while the other enjoys attending the opera and listens to classical music then you will probably have an issue.

- Desire to watch movies that are uplifting and clean with no partial or full nudity, curse words, blood and gore or anything that could grieve the Holy Spirit. When a person exposes themselves or their loved ones to movies that are not clean or pure then the scenes in those movies will play over and over again in their minds and memories.

- You encourage and lift each other up consistently with no jealousy between anyone. You put each other's desires ahead of your own often. You are genuinely interested in the things that your mate is interested in and not because you want them to agree to marry you and then once married will not support them in their personal goals, but because you truly have an interest.

- Honesty is paramount in a relationship. When you lie and are not forthright you create an environment of distrust and it can affect everything you do for a long time until you earn the trust back. People know if they are doing something that would be considered wrong by their spouse and will attempt to hide it. But once uncovered it will take a long time to repair the damage that was lost. So just be honest if you make a mistake.

- If you have friends of the opposite sex, you never put them ahead of your mate and you only communicate when necessary with them. No private discussions that are not healthy and never hide anything from your mate. Facebook can give easy access for you to chat with other people so you may need to unfriend certain people if they cross the line. You must never allow the enemy to come in through private discussions with people of the opposite sex that could open the door to an emotional soul tie or sexual relationship.

- You are both more happy and uplifted being around each other than being alone. You bring joy, laughter and love to one another when together. You miss each other if you have not spoken to each other for a day.

- Best friends look out for each other regardless if they think you will marry them or not. They will take time and spend it with each other as long as they need to talk. They will not try to see what they can get out of you and what you can do for them. They will not pursue you for selfish sexual gratification.

A best friend will want what is best for you, even if it causes them to not spend as much time with you as they used to. They have your best interests at heart even when they have nothing to gain. Many people say that a man and a woman cannot be just good friends because eventually it will lead to a desire for more, such as marriage or a sexual relationship. Since I have become single for really the first time in my life (the Lord had me remarry so quickly that I did not have time to know what it was like to be single before), I have learned a lot about the life of a single person in today's age.

Single people want to have a person that they can hang out with at times. Often times they have to relearn how to be at peace by themselves and not lonely. Single people often eat alone and should always sleep alone. The enemy will try to tempt and lure you into things that are not healthy so you have to keep your guard up at all times and not have even an appearance of sin in your life. No compromising ever. I have ministered to thousands of mostly single (and some married) women around the world and have learned that what they really want is unconditional love and someone to listen to them share their heart. But I must make sure to maintain a healthy relationship that does not go to a level that is not professional. I could never have received the insight that I learned had I been married because the depth of the conversations would never have been appropriate. Now I feel like I have thousands of sisters around the world that can have a safe, healthy conversation about the very real struggles that they are having with being alone and wanting a man. I have also learned how so many men are not pure and godly and just want a quick fix to having a sexual release. There also are many good men out there who have been attracted to women who were not to be trusted. This season of my life was invaluable in the writing of this book because I never could have received such inside information had I not gone through being single. I now know exactly what it feels like to return to the single world.

There is nothing in the world like finding a real and honest person who has nothing to hide and wants to love you unconditionally. A true friend wants nothing but your best interest at heart, whether you will marry them or not. It is a rare thing to find a true friend but if you are patient, do not rush things into your own timing, and allow the Lord to finish working on you while at the same time working on your future spouse, then you can find each other and be married for a lifetime of love and peace with no arguments.

Best friends will usually have a lot in common that they will not have to change to become who the other person wants them to be. In other words, let's say a man has a desire to help people get set free from enemy spirits and is in a ministry where he is being blessed by the Lord. A potential mate would also have the same desire and may be operating in that same type of ministry part time where she is at in her life. The Lord would then bring them together and then they may ultimately start ministering together in the future. They will both have hearts to help love on people who are hurting and want them to be set free. There is nothing more amazing then for a man and a woman to have a strong desire to minister to people together. I would venture to say that it is even a better, longer lasting feeling then sexual intercourse, because sex is a short lived feeling while ministering together for hours, days, weeks, months and years will tie people together in such a way that knits their spirits as one more tightly than ever. Yes, sexual intercourse between two godly people who do not have the spirits of Jezebel or Ahab is amazing and truly intimate, but ministering for hours together as a team each day over many months and years is on another playing field that few couples get to enjoy.

Therefore, there is something very right about finding someone who you enjoy being around and talking to and actually miss not being around. If you get tired of their talking or mannerisms before you get married you will get very annoyed living around them 24 hours a day. So become a good friend to them and allow the Lord to slowly bring things together over time. Rushing into a marriage is usually a recipe for disaster because your future spouse is able to mask any negatives in their behavior over a short time but will find it very challenging to hide it over a year or more. The more time you remain best friends, the more likely you will have a great marriage in the long run.

Friendships that are healthy will be very easy to want to be around the person and spend time talking and being together. They take no effort on both parties and there should always be laughter and fun present. Laughter is good for the soul and sadness and depression makes a person sick. Therefore look to be friends with someone who brings life and not death when you are around them.

Best friends never yell or get mean and angry or want to control each other. When you have a friendship, you will need to treat the other person with love and respect and kindness or else you will not be able to maintain the friendship as your mate will simply end it. The same principle applies to marriage. Discern if the person is really having a hard time just being a friend to you and thus is wearing a mask to cover up who they really are inside. If they are at peace and not anxious, then they are usually showing you who they really are and are not being someone that you want them to be. Anxiety and fear are always present in a person who operates in the Jezebel spirit. They do not want you to see who they really are inside. Best friends do not need to look over their shoulder to see if you will find out that they lied to you about something. They are honest and kind.

Taking time to get to know a person is the best way to see what the person will be like when they are going through hard times, stressful situations, and challenges. If they are going to be a good mate then they will be there for you during the tough times and they will treat you with love and respect throughout those challenging times. If you can spend a full year with someone on a regular basis then you should be able to see how they handle themselves when things are going well and when things may be a little bumpy. The longer period of time that you spend with them the less easy it will be for a person to hide who they really are.

Best friends will not take an offense over and over again. Those who are offended easily are not going to be your best friend and will usually end up being a very poor mate. When someone takes an offense they are off and put up a fence around themselves. It is best to leave them alone to have their own pity party because if you feel sorry for them then you are playing to what that spirit on them wants you to do. Proverbs 19:11 ESV states, "Good sense makes one slow to anger, and it is his glory to overlook an offense."

Best friends are there for you at any hour of the night. If you need help they will be there when you need them. They will not complain at you or blame you for everything that is wrong. They will love you unconditionally. They will not drain you of energy and cause you to feel smothered by them. They will be there with you hand in hand walking down the street or path, watching the sunset together in the mountains or on the beach, and never causing strife in words. You will feel peace around them at most all times and never feel threatened. You will want to talk to them when you go to sleep and cannot wait to hear their voice when you wake up the next morning. They will tell you that they love you and really mean it, not using it as a ploy to get you to do what they want. Proverbs 18:24 NKJV, "A man who has friends must himself be friendly, But there is a friend who sticks closer than a brother."

Chapter 7

Courting Best Practices

Once you have a potential mate identified as healthy, godly and the one that you think you would like to marry, what should you do during the season of courtship. You are basically changing from living a life of singleness to living a life of sharing your time, money and experiences with another in hopefully a more fulfilling way. Remaining sexually pure before the Lord is now top priority at this stage. The reason for this is because if you were to allow yourselves to have any type of impure sexual relationship, then the enemy will be able to use it against you and the Lord will not be able to protect and bless you until later after true repentance. The enemy can convict you in the courtrooms of heaven and the Lord cannot override it because you are guilty. Also those who have stumbled in a premarital sexual relationship will always feel like they have let the Lord down, even though He can forgive you if you truly repent later. There is something so special about waiting until you say "I do" to have the excitement level and anticipation of a very special wedding night and honeymoon. So what are the best practices to use during the time of courtship? I have listed several below that the Lord has advised me to adhere to:

- Stay clear from any sexual contact at all times. No touching of any body parts that are off limits (touching legs in places you know are too close to stimulating other private parts, breasts, etc).

- For me personally I will not even kiss the other person on the lips before marriage because if I do, it will cause each of us to desire more because the logical next step to kissing is touching other body parts and eventually concluding with sexual intercourse. Kissing a person's cheek is fine but once you move to the lips or mouth, it becomes much more intimate and will fire up your sexual engine and to stop it will become much harder as time progresses as you will justify and excuse things. I remember with my second wife how special it was to tell the people who attended our wedding that they would be witnessing our first kiss on the mouth ever and they were amazed as it was such a good pure feeling because it showed to others that I would not compromise myself sexually in any way possible. It was such a special moment.

- If you have been married previously many justify that having sex before marriage is ok because you have already had it – this is absolutely not right and is sin. Never compromise what the Lord has set as a standard because there will be consequences to any kind of premarital sex. You will feel guilty and not pure before the Lord and you do not want that on your conscious before being married.

- You should never talk coarsely about sex, sending any partial nudity or more explicit pictures or videos to each other before marriage as that will allow the enemy to hurt you spiritually and cause your fleshly desires to take center stage which will draw you into sin. Never compromise your integrity for anyone.

- Do godly things together such as worshipping at church, praying together both in your native language but also in tongues. Praying in tongues together is even more intimate then sexual intercourse as it is completely pure in the spirit and you feel spiritually as one on a level unlike any other. When you pray in tongues you cannot argue, hate or otherwise taint the relationship.

- Be careful as to what movies you watch because there is so much that grieves the Holy Spirit that you should not ever watch. Watching Christian and uplifting movies with a positive message are fine. However, doing more interactive activities where you talk is even healthier than watching a lot of movies.

- Going for walks around lakes, on paths, hiking in the woods or forests are definitely good where you can hold hands and reveal who you are to each other at a deeper and real level. Be totally transparent and honest with each other because when you hold back the truth, and later it comes out, you will be sorry that you concealed it.

- Riding bikes, roller blading, driving on short excursions are fun as it is life giving to go on a new adventure to see where you arrive. God created us to have adventures and surprises in life.

- Kayaking and canoeing on rivers or lakes are also fun where you can maneuver and take a joint adventure in water. You can also take a picnic lunch or dinner with you.

- Street ministry is always fun to do – so go to a mall or other event and look for people that the Holy Spirit highlights and prophesy over them, pray for their healings, and just love on them together. There is something so very special when you minister together. If your potential spouse wants nothing to do with these godly activities you will see a red flag go up and you must not ignore it.

- Listening to live music is also a good way to relax and just enjoy life with a person who you are learning more about. Some people like to dance which is definitely a great way of learning what each other is comfortable with prior to marriage.

- Taking short trips to different state parks or national parks is a fun adventure and you can see how each other behaves during various situations, who wants to try various paths or roads to see where they lead. Life should be a series of different adventures in order to let the Holy Spirit lead you to various surprises along the way.

When you spend more time together it is so important to stay pure sexually because the enemy will be trying his best to cause you to stumble. Therefore, when you are put in positions of alone time you must be so very careful not to allow touching each other inappropriately as it could lead to the wrong thing. If you are in each other's home or apartment then make sure you do not stay past a certain time (like 11:00 pm or midnight) when you get tired and your spirit is weaker as your flesh will gain strength against it. This could cause you to want to just "sleep over" on the couch and then before you know it you are both in the same bed doing something that will cause you to sin and then you will feel guilty and condemned afterwards. Never compromise purity.

Therefore talk about the ground rules so you are both on the same page and then do not compromise when one person is weaker than the other. Most times the man will want to compromise sexually but sometimes women are the weaker one. Praying in tongues together often will strengthen both of your spirits to do the right thing over your flesh. If you do not have your prayer language to pray in tongues I strongly encourage you to ask the Lord for that gift. One of the most notable men who has ever lived is quoted in the Word of God as saying, "I thank my God I speak with tongues more than you all," (1 Corinthians 14:18 NKJV). This was the incredible Apostle Paul who declared how important speaking in tongues was and if a man who wrote more of the New Testament than any other thought it was important enough to pray in tongues more than anyone else, then what do you think that says to the rest of the world? The tenacious Peter also spoke in tongues and ministered this experience to others everywhere he went as it was key to getting as many believers to become activated in the Spirit so that they could do the same miracles, signs and wonders like all of the other disciples did. Those gifts did not just die out with the few disciples or those at Pentecost, they continued on in the lives of all Christians that wanted all the gifts available to them to this day. Even the most important man of all – Jesus Christ, prophesied, "they shall speak with new tongues," (Mark 16:17) so if Jesus said it then you better believe it because that settles it for me. Of course the enemy would not want you to speak in tongues because if you do you will be able to reign over him in power and authority and defeat his tactics at every turn. The enemy would want you to believe that it was only for the disciples, or that it was actually from the enemy which is so ridiculous.

Simply speaking, Peter and Paul benefited enormously by speaking in tongues. These two dynamic men of God, as recorded in the Scriptures, paint a moving example for the reader of what impactful of a role praying in tongues played in their life. Thus, if they spent so much time talking about the benefits of it in the Word, then you can expect that we all better be doing it in order to be fully and completely activated to do what Jesus did. Do you want to be halfway armed to fight the enemy or do you want to be fully armed? Do you want to allow the enemy to beat you at every turn and live a defeated life in your future marriage and life or do you want to put him on the run everywhere you go. It is time to put on the full armor which includes praying in tongues every day for the rest of your life to cause the enemy to run from you. So if you have never received your prayer language yet, ask for it now and expect the Lord to give you what is good for you.

If you can just envision Jesus sitting beside you or walking with you and how you would want to appear before him with your mate at all times it really helps to guide you. When you feel very close to the Lord then it becomes extremely hard to have a fleshly desire that would cause him to be sad. I remember hearing Todd White talking back in 2015 in Elkhart, IN and he said something along the lines that he no longer had a desire to sin because it was no longer attractive anymore. That is exactly how I now feel because my heart has been changed into more of Jesus' heart. I have no desire to sin because it is not appealing in the least. I used to struggle with sexual purity many years ago but not anymore because why would I want to compromise what I know the Lord would have me do. I love the Lord so much that I never would want to make him sad. There is something so freeing about walking in purity every day and night, doing what the Lord wants us to do.

Chapter 8

Healthy Communications

When having communications with someone who is going to be your future husband and wife, it is very important to think before you speak. There are so many people who excuse themselves by saying that they just 'speak their minds.' Unfortunately much of what is in their mind is not from the Lord as the enemy has been speaking to them all their lives. Therefore, they must retrain their old faulty mindsets to be slow to speak and quick to hear as well as to discern what they are hearing in their minds. So much of what a person thinks is not their own thoughts but the enemy's voice and they have listened to the enemy most of their life so they just speak out the words that they are hearing. This causes much strife in one's life as they offend people often and then take an offense easily.

It is critical that you think before you speak and discern how your mate will receive it. If you or your mate has been hurt a lot by your mother or father, the enemy will have spoken to you much of your life. If you speak certain words to your mate that they are not ready to deal with yet, you will receive a harsh word back and can damage your relationship. For instance, if a woman grew up with feeling rejected, criticized and controlled by her father, she will usually have a lot of anger inside of her. She may tend to offend people all day long while becoming enraged if you state one gentle word of correction to her. Therefore you will need to be very careful as to what you say to her. She may not be able to receive any correction at all so if you say a word she does not like then she will take an offense and become angry with you. Thus if you think before you speak, and then bite your tongue and swallow what you were going to say, then you can wait until later for her to receive what you are saying. It may take her weeks, months or even years to receive what you were going to say in love, due to the amount of pain she received over her life and the strength of any enemy spirits that have a right to her.

Often times a person has been hurt so much by their father (or mother) that they really cannot receive any correction whatsoever. So you may have to suffer awhile in loving them like Christ loved the church. I wrote a book called *Loving Like Christ : How to Love the Hard to Love People* which is an excellent resource in learning how to have strong grace for a hurting person and how to view them like Christ. Whatever you say must be covered in extreme love for them to receive it and if you say anything that causes them to feel judged they could become enraged with you, as it will remind them of their father (or mother).

Therefore, one must always be thinking ahead, as to how their mate will receive what they are going to say. Sometimes you simply must say something that they will not want to hear, but you need to always cover it in love, sometimes a lot of love. If they know you are saying it in love they can often times sense that and then will not become angry with you. I have ministered to thousands around the world who have the Jezebel and Leviathan spirits and they have been accustomed to taking an offense at the drop of a hat. But I have only seen a handful of the thousands that could not receive the words I had for them concerning operating out of the spirits of Jezebel and Leviathan. It is called discernment, tact and godly wisdom.

Many people today send short messages through texts or Facebook Messenger, Instagram or other venues. The enemy will often try to speak to the recipient a twisted interpretation in their head of what you innocently intended. Think about this….you may text your mate to see if they want to either spend time together walking at a park or riding their bike. Then your mate responds with "idc or I don't care." You may misinterpret their intention when you read it that "they could care less of doing either thing with you" and then you take an offense and get upset and want nothing to do with them anymore. But in their mind they meant that they would love to do either with you and decided to allow you to make the decision. The enemy often tries to steal, kill and destroy our relationships through misinterpretation of communications, so it is important that we are clear so as to stop any strife that could start.

So when you think about how man communicated in the early stages of this world, it was always in person, so you could read their body language in addition to their voice fluctuations and tones. Then the phone eventually was invented which lost the ability for us to see body language (although we do have video chat today), then texting and now social media. So many relationships have been hurt through confusion of the intention of what was actually being attempted to be communicated by the speaker. The enemy does a good job of doing that every day in this world and we need to pay attention to how the enemy twists communication to alleviate all strife as much as possible.

Therefore, it is always best to take time to talk face to face with each other instead of mainly through texts or even phone calls. The more time you practice communicating in person prior to marriage the more you will really know that person's spirit and have a higher trust level once married. You will also know if you really like being around them or not. So many couples, once married, drift apart into hanging out with their guy or gal friends and then lament who they married.

If people take an offense often, cause strife during dating and are just not fun to be around, then you probably do not want to move forward in marriage. I will never take an offense against anyone and never strive with anyone, ever. People cannot understand how that is possible but since January 23, 2015 I have never had an argument with anyone. If I am talking to someone who is "off" and has the enemy on them in a strong way, I will simply excuse myself from their presence or the phone so as not to engage in an argument. Arguing about anything seems so foreign to me now. When a person has the enemy affecting them strongly they will try to provoke you to anger, or control and manipulate you or cause you to lose your peace. You simply cannot go there with them or you will be pulled into the argument and lose your peace. You must "get out of dodge" and walk away from the person gently. It is so important to keep yourself in peace at all times because once you are on the enemy's territory you will not have peace. So just say no and walk away in love.

If you have the enemy on you and are hearing thoughts from the enemy to cause you to get angry, you need to recognize you are not comfortable and walk away from the situation and pray. Command the enemy to be gone from you in Jesus name. Then come back together with your mate and talk in peace. Whenever you are not in peace it is always the enemy that is affecting you. What are some of the things you can do to communicate in healthier ways?

- Be calm and at peace when talking or texting. Out of that peace you will state things that are more likely to be received by your mate. But be aware that when you text that the enemy can cause a twist to the receiver as to how you intended it. Often times if you can send them a Voice Note (or Voice Message) it would be better than a text because then they will hear your voice and how you meant it.

- Always talk in a loving tone or manner. If you speak in a condescending or mocking tone the recipient will pick up on it and become defensive. When you cover what you say in love it will be received in love. There are thousands of personal deliverance sessions that I have had with people who operated in the Jezebel spirit. The top thing they said to me after getting delivered is that they could feel the love and gentleness of Christ on what I was saying which caused them to receive what I said instead of taking an offense and leaving. They could literally feel the love that I had inside of me for them as I shared the truth.

- When you genuinely desire to love a person like Christ loved the church you have no desires in you to control, manipulate or hurt them. You have no ulterior motive other than to help and encourage them. Therefore, when you are having discussions with someone you will always lift them up and love them in a way that they will feel special and cherished.

- You should be very wary of talking when you are tired at night because usually one person is a night owl while the other is up at the crack of dawn. So you have to be cognizant of that fact because when a person is tired they may not be fully aware of what they are hearing or saying.

- Never communicate when you feel hungry or angry (hangry) because what you say or text will be done out of irritation or impatience and you will say or do things that cause your mate to be hurt. It may then take days or weeks to come back to rebuilding the trust again

- Laughing together in communication is fun and should be done often. When you can look at a situation that may be somewhat serious with a humorous side it really takes the potential for offense out of the picture. I can imagine that Jesus had a lot of fun with Peter on many occasions with all the time that Peter stuck his foot in his mouth.

- Holding hands when talking is always a good, gentle way of having any serious conversation because the person will feel your love for them and receive more easily what they are saying.

-   Writing love notes and leaving it in a place where your mate will find it is usually received as a special thing because very few communicate that way anymore. In fact, if you can write a letter and give it to them or let them find it in their car with an encouraging word in it, you will often cause anticipation with your mate to be excited to read what is inside. It is heartfelt and creates a tenderness of love feeling.

Chapter 9

Never Striving

2 Timothy 2:23-26 NKJV states "[23] But avoid foolish and ignorant disputes, knowing that they generate strife. [24] And a servant of the Lord must not quarrel but be gentle to all, able to teach, patient, [25] in humility correcting those who are in opposition, if God perhaps will grant them repentance, so that they may know the truth, [26] and that they may come to their senses and escape the snare of the devil, having been taken captive by him to do his will." This speaks to the fact that the enemy is behind all strife. If you are ever feeling compelled to speak harshly to your mate it is always the enemy that is behind it - whispering to one or both people trying to get them to either offend someone, take an offense, be selfish, etc. It is ridiculous for a mature Christian to ever argue in marriage. It is always the enemy that is whispering to them in their mind and then

they will unleash a verbal barrage on their mate driving a wedge between them. It is fine to have a calm and civil disagreement with your mate and then have a healthy discussion to find agreement and resolution of the issue.

I personally refuse to strive with anyone ever. It is not possible for me to do so anymore because it is not in my heart to be able to do it. So many people have not learned how to stop strife in their relationships and they need to learn it before they get married to anyone. Much of what they need to do is actually simple. They just need to bite their tongues and speak nothing out of their mouth when they know it will cause an argument to break out. Yes, the tongue is like a rudder and is the hardest thing to bridle and control, but it can and must be done if you are going to have a successful marriage.

I recommend practicing before marriage by thinking before you speak as to how the recipient will receive the words you are about to release. If you can consciously think about "If I were to state X, they will respond with Y" and if you believe they will receive what you say, then you will not have strife or at the most you will just have minimal pushback. But if what you are going to say to someone you suspect without a shadow of a doubt that they will become very agitated or angry about, then it is probably better left unsaid. So think before you speak, every day, every hour and every minute of the day and be aware of how the person will receive what you are going to say. Jesus was very purposeful with every word that He spoke. Life and death is in the power of our tongues, so speak life, not strife.

Now we do not want to go to the extreme and just let our mate bowl us over and go along with everything they want or say that is unhealthy or sinful because then you would be operating in the Ahab spirit. The spirit of Ahab causes you to just turn your head the other way and be taken into sin or other decisions that are not godly. I am talking about not purposefully bringing up a subject that you know will cause your mate to become angry. Too many people excuse themselves by saying "That's just the way I am, so deal with it!" which is not a godly attitude whatsoever. You are held accountable for what you say and how you behave by the Lord. If you are aware of what you are saying or doing will cause another person to become agitated and not comfortable and then choose to do it anyway, then you are sinning.

It can be a definite challenging process of renewing your old mindsets of the past. If you grew up in your family that whoever spoke the loudest and got the angriest got their way, then it could be very foreign to you to speak lovingly and maybe having to sacrifice and not get your way all the time. Marriage is often times about sacrificing your own self-serving desires for another person. You should definitely have healthy discussions on the following areas before getting married to avoid surprises a week or months after being married:

- Which type of church should you both attend together?

- How much to tithe to the church or a ministry (10% of gross income for example)?

- What school to send your children to (Christian, home, or public)? This is a big decision and you need to agree on what education your children will receive.

- How to discipline your children, especially if you will have step children as you will definitely be tested over this when you are a step parent.

- What type of food to eat (healthy, balanced, junk) because you will be what you eat? If you have a wife that wants to eat healthy and a husband that wants to eat junk – this will become a point of contention.

- How much to exercise (daily, weekly, never) and if you will exercise together or separately and at what time of the day?

- What time of the day to get up and go to sleep (most couples have one person who is a night owl and one person who is an early riser)?

- What kind of clothes will you wear or buy? Will you purchase the latest fashions from the mall or the cheapest from Goodwill. Finances are common to have disagreements over so it is important to be open and honest about these discussions. Usually one person is a saver and the other is a spender.

- What are your methods for being healed when sick and staying healthy? (God, doctors, prescription medications, etc).

- Praying in tongues – do you both have this gift and if so praying every day together for several minutes will be the best use of your time as it draws you together spiritually.

- How to handle a disagreement the healthy way (talking it out calmly with reasons instead of who yells the loudest, wins)?

- Paying cash for a car versus financing it (my recommendation is always to pay with cash and then save up for your next car and pay cash for that one).

- Views on living on credit cards or trusting the Lord for provision and living on what you make.

- Will you both keep working at the same jobs or doing ministry together or one doing ministry and one working or one working and one staying at home. Also, what happens if you have children – will the wife stay home to raise the children when they are young.

- Relationships with previous friends of the opposite sex (is it healthy to continue to have discussions with people of the opposite sex after marriage or should you end most of those relationships).

- Traveling together or apart – how often and for what length of time and for what purpose. If one person has a job that takes them on the road often – you should discuss the dynamics of how it will play out with the family.

- How do you both get directed from the Lord as you want to make sure that both are hearing from the Lord and if you both hear a different word or get different direction then who makes the final call (husband usually should make the final decision assuming he is a believer and hears the Lord, since he answers to God).

- What does the Bible mean when it says "Wives Should Submit to Their Husbands" in Ephesians 5:22? Obviously if you have a loving and godly husband this will not be an issue. But if the husband has a Jezebel spirit and is very controlling and mean then you simply cannot allow yourself to be abused.

- What does the Bible mean when it says "Husbands, love your wives, just as Christ also loved the church and gave Himself for her" in Ephesians 5:25? It definitely is a challenge but if a husband is married to a wife with the controlling Jezebel spirit, he must not submit himself to abuse but for a season in order to get her eventually set free.

- Prophetic words from the Lord from your spouse and others – receiving advice from friends who do not hear from the Lord may be different from those who do hear reliably from the Lord. So who will you go to in order to get wisdom and advice after you are married?

- What kind of fun activities do you each enjoy doing – often times a mate will act like they enjoy what you like to do before marriage but then once they have you they will change their minds and admit they really do not like it.

- How much time spent with friends – this can be a real point of contention so discuss what is a reasonable amount of time to spend with your friends separate from your mate.

- Hobbies and how much time devoted to it – some men spend all their spare time on their hobbies and some women want to go shopping often. Discuss how much time you will spend with your hobbies.

When you talk about these issues prior to marriage you know what to expect, to some level, of what you will get during marriage. It is best going into a marriage with knowing what you are dealing with then hours after you say "I do" having your spouse trying to stop you when you want to go to Dairy Queen an enjoy an occasional Blizzard dessert after dinner and you are like…. "Didn't see that coming…."

This will reduce the amount of strife greatly in your marriage because then you will know what the agreed upon expectations were before you married. The key to all of this is being open and honest. Those with very strong Jezebel spirits will lie to your face telling you what they think you want to hear in order to get you to marry them. So again, if you take your time and stretch it out to over a year of dating / courting and then get engaged to be married, you will better be able to pick up on who they really are behind closed doors when no one else is within earshot. People who have the

Jezebel spirit at a strong level will be extremely deceiving to lure you in, so you must be on your spiritual discernment game in order to know for yourself before it is too late.

Strife in a marriage is definitely an intimacy killer and needs to be stopped in its tracks. Strife leads to all kinds of evil and negative things in a marriage. I remember when I was in Jerusalem attending a two week tour of Israel with my wife and we could hear the couple in the room next door to us. We knew who they were and they were a large supporter of the ministry that we were on the trip with. They said some very mean words to each other every day and night and it just grieved my spirit to hear them argue and strive. The only thing I could do was to walk out of the room to get away from it. Every time we saw that couple on the trip they were striving. Then back home in the United States we saw them at various conference striving all the time but then her husband stopped coming to the events. Eventually they got a divorce. When a couple strives all kinds of evil from the enemy has a right to come in and torment them. So everyone needs to take this seriously and never let a harsh, critical, judgmental or angry word leave their lips. Just say no to strife.

Chapter 10

After You Say 'I Do'

Once you have officially gotten married to your Prince Charming or Princess Cinderella - what will happen next is that you will begin to learn what life will really be like living with them as both of your guards will now be completely let down. If you both have followed what I have written in this book you hopefully are loving your new life of joint marital bliss. As much as you hope that what you are getting is the real deal, there are usually things that the person will do which will cause you to pause and think "Hmmmm....wonder what else will not be the same?" It is funny (or not) what happens once a person feels that they finally have you. I know many who have been married to someone before who will often hold their breath in the weeks or months after they get remarried to see if they got sold a bill of goods that was false advertising. They will have their fingers crossed hoping that their new husband or wife will not control or manipulate them. Or they will try to enforce their way of life on their new mate and become upset if they don't get their way. If a person has been set freed from the spirits of Jezebel and Ahab, then their marriage should be much more peaceful and enjoyable. But if they still have some remnants of those spirits inside due to pain from their fathers or mothers, then it could be a bumpy road, which is never fun.

So what should the first few months of the new marriage look like? What can you do to help ease into the new pattern of having to sacrifice some of the things that you used to be able to do on your own with now allowing another person to dictate some of the decisions?

- You should be slow to speak and quick to listen, and never control your spouse or strive about anything with them because it will hurt your relationship. Be loving, gentle and sweet at all times. Treat the other person like they are a gift from God (because they are!).

- You should be willing to spend time with your new bride or bridegroom and learn sexually about each other in a healthy way. Men should desire to make sure their wives receive satisfaction sexually and then they will be satisfied in return by their wives. Always be sensitive and caring about each other's needs.

- You should spend more time laughing and loving then you do complaining and crying. Humor is a good thing and definitely should be a significant part of a person's life because God wants you to have fun. The enemy wants you to be serious, selfish, fearful, angry and sad.

- Continue to take time to date each other by setting aside at least one night a week. Keep your marriage fun and enjoy each other's interests. Alternate dates between what you want to do and what your spouse wants to do. This is supposed to be fun – you each will learn how to sacrifice what your personal desires are for each other.

- Pray together every day and pray in tongues at least 15 minutes together as well. Remember when you pray in tongues you come together much closer in the spirit and your spirits will get stronger against your flesh while you are prophesying your future. Plus you cannot hear the enemy whispering to you when you pray in tongues.

- Merge your bank accounts together because the enemy would like nothing more than to take sides – you should have the mindset that you are now one. No prenuptial agreements allowed because that is set up to allow the enemy to keep that in the back of your mind. One man's wife had him refinance her home mortgage (where her sons lived and paid a discounted rent). She purposefully left his name off of the ownership of the home on the refinanced home, but yet included him as owing on it. He signed the refinancing papers and didn't think twice about it because he loved her like Christ. Unfortunately later she filed for divorce and said that he didn't have any legal ownership of the home even though he had been paying for all of the mortgage and most of the utilities for her sons. She had not gotten set free from the spirits of Jezebel and Leviathan so was still doing things covertly to protect herself instead of completely giving herself together to him. She also opened up a private bank account of her own about a year before they separated as she was preparing to divorce him secretly as she had gone through three times before. He had taken on over $85,000 worth of her sons living expenses and debts and didn't think twice because they were now his sons. We must get into the mindset that our individual money is now ours together or the enemy will use it to destroy us.

- Worship together both in the corporate environment at church or a ministry as well as privately. Crank up the Christian music at home or the car and sing together and get your praise on. There is nothing like singing and worshiping with your spouse songs from the Lord.

If you begin to have issues where one person or both are getting into strife then one or both of you are being hit by the enemy. It is so critical to identify where your thoughts are coming from and to shut down the enemy. All strife comes from the enemy and needs to be stopped or else it will lead to the deterioration of the marriage. I am reprinting from my book *Keep Your Peace On* what you should do if strife has escalated past the point that you can't take it anymore:

The best thing to do when strife has escalated past the point that you can take it is to part. Pray, Assess, Return, Together. If someone is attacking you and will not relent then the best thing to do is tell them that you need to separate for the moment. The length of time for the moment may be just for ten or fifteen minutes in order to get to a place of safety, quiet and peace again. You may just have to walk away from the person into an adjacent room or bathroom. Or you may need to walk from your kitchen to an upstairs or basement bedroom. If the aggressive person who is verbally attacking you wants to follow you wherever you go then you may need to run outside or get in your car and leave. I have experienced where the person tried to stop me from leaving by standing behind my car in the garage or driveway prohibiting me from leaving and chasing me into another room and that can make it especially challenging to get away. Persevere as much as you are able because as long as that person is operating out of the enemy spirit on them trying to control you they will verbally barrage you with no relenting. It is obviously not healthy for your spirit to be around them and you need to "get out of Dodge."

PRAY. Once you are safely apart from your family member the first thing to do is to pray. Declare out loud to come against the enemy spirit on your spouse, child or family member. Speak out something like, "I command the enemy to be shut down, and bind and rebuke him from (name) in the name of Jesus!" and "I declare that (name) is at peace and is calm and will only speak words of love from their mouth!" Remember that even though your family member may be getting hit by the enemy that you also have an authority as a believer and can help them by going to war against the enemy for them. Ultimately they need to get their peace back by calming down and realizing that they have been hit by the enemy and it may take them several hours to get their peace back. Understand that the same authority that you have to command healing like Jesus did is the same authority you carry over demonic forces as well. The other person does have a free will and if they continue to stay angry and speak out enemy words it may take them much longer to come back to a calmer state. Pray for their eyes to be opened and scales removed to what the enemy is doing to them.

If you have your prayer language (and I highly recommend everyone to ask the Lord for it if they do not have it) then praying in tongues will bring you back into a state of peace very quickly. Pray as long as it takes for you to be in peace. Therefore it could be just five minutes or it could take as long as thirty minutes to keep the enemy from speaking to you. Praying in tongues is praying the perfect prayer and when you declare words out loud that are perfect you change the atmosphere and more rapidly get your peace back and break down the enemy on and around others.

ASSESS. Assess means to determine what state of mind that your family member is in after you have prayed for them. How long do you stay apart from your loved one? The Holy Spirit can direct you as to what the state of mind that your loved one is in and if they are calm again yet. Sometimes it may only take fifteen minutes while other times it may take an hour or several hours. You may need to text the person to test the waters to what state of mind that they are in. If they continue to text you back words of harshness or strife then you should stay away longer because the enemy is still affecting them. You can let them know that you will come back when they are calm again so they are not afraid that you will not come back. A woman that has endured many relationships or marriages where her husband or men left her will need to be reassured that you will come back or else the enemy will whisper to them that they are going to lose another man again and their fear will escalate to try to tighten their grip over their husband. Also if your family member tries to call you over and over in rapid succession then you will know that they are not at peace and you need to stay away longer until their behavior is consistent with being peaceful.

I knew one woman who was so scared of her father and brother that she allowed them to berate her on the phone for over an hour blaming her for everything and making her feel more hurt and was unable to hang up and let them know she needed to go. She said that if she did not take the verbal abuse and hung up that they would call her back over and over until she answered and then really let her have it. The enemy spirit on someone can be extreme in every way imaginable but you must stand up for yourself to protect you from further harsh treatment and to come against the enemy in your family member. Eventually they will learn that they can no longer abuse you and make you do what they want and will have to treat you with respect. It may take several months or years of training them before they understand that you will not allow the control and abuse any longer.

So the proper assessment of the status of your loved one should be taken after you have prayed and given them time to calm down into a state of peace again. Once you have determined sufficiently that they are now at peace again you are safe to then return.

RETURN. Once you have assessed that your family member is back at peace you can return to them. When you return you need to be careful that your family member has not lied to you only to get you to come back so they can verbally abuse you again. So return only after you are confident as much as you can be that they are now at peace again. When returning it is best to approach them carefully because if they lied only to get you to come back so they could really let you have it again verbally, then you need to part again and you may want to stay away overnight for your safety and to teach them how to tell the truth to you. If they are safely at peace then stay in love towards them and never speak any words of condemnation to them or scolding. Respond to them with the love of the Father and speak only kind, loving and gentle words that the Lord would have you say. It would be good to help them see that when they "lost it" that the enemy was behind it all and not them. They are not a "bad person" but the enemy was very bad in trying to cause strife between you. When you can consistently connect them with how the enemy gave them a thought and then they spoke it out instead of saying how you were hurt by them then they can receive it much better. When you equate that they were being used by the enemy and thus they lost their peace then they can start to realize that it was true and eventually you can teach them about commanding the spirits to go from them whenever they are starting to lose their peace. If they will not receive you then it may be time to part again because you do not want to return only to start hearing them strive again. Once they have stayed in their peace for an hour or so and can talk to you calmly it would be good to spend a little time together in that peace.

TOGETHER. Being together after an episode of strife is a good thing because it reassures the person that you love them and want to help them stay in peace. You can spend time walking outside in nature which usually brings a person into more peace or you may just hold each other and hug them reiterating that you love them and you both must help each other to realize that it is always the enemy that causes one of you to lose your peace. After an enemy attack it is always good to pray together and if you both have your prayer language I would recommend praying in tongues for at least ten to fifteen minutes as this ushers in more peace unlike anything that you could do. The more that you can move back into the peaceful Spirit mode, away from the flesh, the better. Praying in the Spirit shuts down the enemy from any backlash of being able to speak to your spouse or family member. Since you have been apart for a significant amount of time you should try to spend time together enjoying something together for at least an hour or more depending on the amount of time that you were apart.

There may come a time that you simply must separate for a season from someone that is being affected by the enemy in a strong way because the enemy will try to shut you down especially if you are involved in ministry. If so, ask the Lord if you are to separate and He will confirm it to you. The purpose of separation will be to help your loved one to deal with the spirits that are afflicting them in order to get freed. They should work with a Holy Spirit led counselor who hears from the Lord to provide insight to them as to what has gone on in their lives and then be able to help them get delivered. You will need to stay at a safe, peaceful place in order to recover from the attacks. If the person will not admit that they have any areas to be delivered from or to work on and want to keep the spirits and thus the horrible behaviors then you need to ask the Lord what He would have you do next. You should concentrate on drawing closer to the Lord through this separation and if you are separated from your spouse make sure to not allow the enemy to tempt you to confide closely with a person from the opposite sex that could be unhealthy in an emotional or physical sense as this could open up an entirely new issue to deal with. Stay pure before the Lord at all times.

Parting should be done as long as the person continues to be over the top when it comes to their reactions or behaviors towards you and have minimal desire to be willing to work on their issues through deliverance or Holy Spirit led counsel. The goal of it is to help train the other person that if they are going to continue to be abusive then you will not tolerate it and will leave. Over time they usually learn to change because they grow weary of being alone and genuinely want healthy companionship. Also they normally will need some deliverance of the spirits that have caused them to behave so aggressively. So they need to seek out a good Holy Spirit led counselor that understands how to get people free from demonic spirits.

If you have done your homework before being married, been successfully delivered from all generational curses, spirits of Jezebel, Leviathan, and Ahab - then you should experience the greaterness of love, respect, peace, joy, laughter and fun in marriage. The Lord wants to bless you with an amazing marriage that others will want what you have. Make the Lord proud of you and enjoy your spouse!

References

The New King James Version of the Bible
The English Standard Version of the Bible

Final Thoughts

Being set free from the enemy is a must when you are trying to choose a godly mate. The enemy will always try to deceive you that spirits are not real and that you should get married to the most physically attractive person you can get. Unfortunately when you grow up with the Ahab spirit affecting you, then you will be drawn to someone with the Jezebel spirit and be setting yourself up for a marriage that will be miserable. If you grew up with the Jezebel spirit then you will not be able to help yourself in starting strife in your marriage. So get freed from all spirits now before you choose to get married or remarried and save yourself from a lifetime of pain and heart ache.

If you would like me to speak and minister at your church, seminar or conference, you may contact me on my website. If the revelations in this book have helped you and changed your life or saved your marriage you may wish to make a tax deductible donation to Restored to Freedom at http://www.restoredtofreedom.com which will help continue to get the message out to people all over the world, that there is hope and a way to gain total freedom in Jesus Christ. Amen.

NOTES

NOTES

<u>NOTES</u>

Made in the USA
Middletown, DE
02 April 2019